PROJECT GARDEN

A MONTH-BY-MONTH GUIDE
to Planting, Growing, and Enjoying
ALL Your Backyard Has to Offer

Stacy Tornio
Master Gardener

Adamsmedia
Avon, Massachusetts

Published by Adams Media,
a division of F+W Media, Inc.
57 Littlefield Street, Avon, MA 02322. U.S.A.
www.adamsmedia.com

Interior design by Elisabeth Lariviere.

ISBN-10: 1-4405-2772-5
ISBN-13: 978-1-4405-2772-2
eISBN-10: 1-4405-2964-7
eISBN-13: 978-1-4405-2964-1

Printed in China.

10 9 8 7 6 5 4 3 2 1

Library of Congress Cataloging-in-Publication Data
is available from the publisher.

This publication is designed to provide accurate and authoritative information with regard to the subject matter covered. It is sold with the understanding that the publisher is not engaged in rendering legal, accounting, or other professional advice. If legal advice or other expert assistance is required, the services of a competent professional person should be sought.
—From a *Declaration of Principles* jointly adopted by a Committee of the American Bar Association and a Committee of Publishers and Associations

Many of the designations used by manufacturers and sellers to distinguish their product are claimed as trademarks. Where those designations appear in this book and Adams Media was aware of a trademark claim, the designations have been printed with initial capital letters.

Readers are urged to take all appropriate precautions before undertaking any how-to task. Always read and follow instructions and safety warnings for all tools and materials, and call in a professional if the task stretches your abilities too far. Although every effort has been made to provide the best possible information in this book, neither the publisher nor the author are responsible for accidents, injuries, or damage incurred as a result of tasks undertaken by readers. This book is not a substitute for professional services.

This book is available at quantity discounts for bulk purchases.
For information, please call 1-800-289-0963.

To my enormously talented mother, Linda, who is an amazing seamstress, crafter, woodworker, and more. Mom, I know I never quite caught on to sewing, but this book proves you've influenced me in many other ways. Thanks.

Acknowledgments

First and foremost, this book wouldn't be possible without my encouraging and wonderful husband, Steve. He's the one who entertained my children and gave me peace for hours upon hours so that I could finish this book. I also want to thank all the friends and family who helped me brainstorm and test these ideas. From Linda, Maggie, and Vicki, who helped me put the finishing touches on many of the projects, to my extended Oklahoma family, who lent me portions of their recipes from our family cookbook, it was a group effort. Also to my talented brother-in-law, Scott, and my best friend, Tina, who both have a natural knack for photography and took some amazing project photos for this book.

In addition, I would like to thank my lovely agent, Uwe Stender of TriadaUS, who always sees the silver lining. And to a talented editor, Victoria Sandbrook, who definitely helped me take this book to the next level.

To all my fellow Master Gardeners out there, thank you for all that you do in our garden communities. Finally, I thank my two kids, Jack and Annabelle. You two are the reason I've become so involved with Kids Gardening programs and activities. Let's go get dirty!

CONTENTS

Introduction ix

JANUARY

Grow It: Plants
Rosemary, Cilantro, Parsley, Basil, Oregano. . . . 2

Plant It.
Soup's On Herb Garden Plan 4

Eat It.
Lovely Lemons 6

Recycle It.
Seed Catalog Art. 9

Make It.
Awesome Aromas 12

Make It.
Plant Markers Made Easy. 14

FEBRUARY

Grow It: Plants
Allium, Snowdrop, Crocus, Iris, Hyacinth 18

Plant It.
Heart Garden Plan 20

Eat It.
Rockin' Radishes. 22

Recycle It.
Food for Birds 26

Recycle It.
Water for the Birds 28

Make It.
Homes for Birds 30

MARCH

Grow It: Plants
Redbud, Lilac, Forsythia, Azalea, Peonies. 34

Plant It.
Purple in Springtime Plan 36

Eat It.
Powerhouse Potatoes. 38

Recycle It.
Seed Starting 41

Make It.
Seed Planting Made Easy. 43

Make It.
Veggies in Containers. 44

APRIL

Grow It: Plants
Butterfly Weed, Catmint, Tiger Lily,
Elephant Ear, Hens and Chicks 46

Plant It.
Flowers and Veggies Plan 48

Eat It.
Creative with Carrots 50

Recycle It.
Add Life to Your Garden 53

Recycle It.
Creative Containers 54

Make It.
DIY Garden Path 57

MAY

Grow It: Plants
Fuchsia, Petunia, Coleus, Marigolds,
Impatiens 60

Plant It.
Prized Petunias Plan 62

Eat It.
Great Green Beans 64

Recycle It.
Serve It Up 66

Recycle It.
Order in the Garden 68

Make It.
Personalized Containers for Your Plants 71

JUNE

Grow It: Plants
Balloon Flower, Daylily, Hosta,
Columbine, Coral Bells 74

Plant It.
Salsa Garden Plan 76

Eat It.
Perfect Peppers 78

Recycle It.
Going on a Bug Hunt 81

Recycle It.
Your Garden's Best Friends 83

Make It.
The Natural Artist 85

JULY

Grow It: Plants
Shasta Daisy, Black-Eyed Susan,
Purple Coneflower, Bee Balm, Garden Phlox . . 88

Plant It.
Patriotic Container Plan 90

Eat It.
Tasty Tomatoes 92

Recycle It.
Decorating in the Garden 95

Make It.
'Tis the Growing Season 99

Make It.
Saving Summer's Splendor 100

AUGUST

Grow It: Plants
Cosmos, Spider Flower, Sunflowers,
Zinnias, Morning Glory 102

Plant It.
Growing Tall Plan. 104

Eat It.
Craving Cucumbers 106

Recycle It.
Games in the Garden 108

Recycle It.
Backyard Tunes .111

Make It.
Veggie Gardening Round II 113

SEPTEMBER

Grow It: Plants
Liatris, Coreopsis, Clematis, Blanket
Flower, Honeysuckle 116

Plant It.
Night Garden Plan .118

Eat It.
Savory Squash 120

Recycle It.
Preserving Food 123

Recycle It.
Harvesting Seeds 125

Make It.
September Flowers 127

OCTOBER

Grow It: Plants
Aster, Ornamental Grass, Tulips,
Mums, Sedum 130

Plant It.
Create a Spooky Garden Plan 132

Eat It.
Yummy Pumpkin Goop 134

Recycle It.
Creative Faces 137

Make It.
Raise a Butterfly 139

Make It.
If They Only Had a Brain 141

NOVEMBER

Grow It: Plants
Daffodils, Knockout Roses, Pansies,
Geraniums, Ornamental Cabbage 144

Plant It.
Welcome Wagon Plan 146

Eat It.
Onions with Attitude 148

Recycle It.
Fun with Leaves 151

Make It.
Gardening in Any Weather 154

Make It.
Multiply Your Plants 156

DECEMBER

Grow It: Plants
Amaryllis, Christmas Cactus, Dwarf
Alberta Spruce, African Violet, Poinsettias 158

Plant It.
Red and Green Display Plan 160

Eat It.
Lovable Lettuce. 162

Recycle It.
Gifts that Keep on Growing 166

Make It.
Let's Get Personal. 168

Make It.
Countdown-till-Spring Calendar 171

General Index. 173
Index of Recipes 179

Introduction

Gardening is one of America's favorite pastimes, and it's quickly growing in popularity among parents, kids, schools, and more. After all, what else gets kids outside, engages them year-round, and helps them get in touch with nature?

No matter where you live or what time of year it is, there are always new ways to introduce your kids to gardening. There are hundreds of age-appropriate activities, and there's always something new to explore—indoors or out! Best of all: it doesn't take an expert gardener to guide children through the nearly 200 projects you'll find in this book. Organized by month, each chapter covers five types of activities that will keep the little nature-lovers in your life growing!

Grow It offers plant recommendations and general gardening advice to make sure you and your kids have instant success. You'll find plants that thrive in sunny yards, shaded patios, northern winters, and southern summers—a little something for everyone.

Plant It illustrates a garden design you can emulate—and makes sure you have all the info you need to keep it looking beautiful. From creative container ideas to fun "animal" or "spooky" themes, there's something here for everyone.

Eat It gives you recipes and ideas for using ingredients from nature to make delicious, healthy foods. So not only do you get great-tasting recipes, but you also get tips for growing that month's featured fruit or veggie.

Recycle It honors the motto of "keep the world beautiful" by using recycled items for unique, nature-related creations. Whether it's an art project like wind chimes or more practical plans like clever ways to start seeds indoors, all ideas are guaranteed to be fun and inexpensive.

Make It has step-by-step, nature-inspired project ideas that will keep your kids busy for hours. All projects are easy to follow and have simple materials, so most can be completed in just an afternoon!

Every project is rated for difficulty, so whether you're just getting started or are already a nature pro, there's something here for everyone. The fewer the spades, the easier it will be to keep a flower in bloom or to whip up a perfect batch of homemade fruit slushies. Throughout the book, little tidbits about plants, gardening, and nature will keep your kids learning a little something extra along the way.

Whether it's rainy or cold, sunny or snowy, there's always something to do, make, and see in your garden. The world is your playground. Get out there and explore!

JANUARY

GROW IT: Plants

There's no doubt about it: January is a wintery month, no matter where you live. But that doesn't mean you can't make headway on your garden this month! Take your green thumb indoors and grow a few herbs instead. They'll be perfect to mix into those warm winter soups.

Rosemary

Difficulty:

The Basics: Perennial, Zones 7 to 10, 24 to 36 inches tall

Grow It: If you live in Zone 7 or higher, plant rosemary in your garden in full sun. If you live in a cooler climate, start the seeds indoors, move the rosemary outside during summer, and bring it back inside as a houseplant during fall and winter. If you can find a rosemary plant instead of starting from seeds, it's definitely worth the investment because they can be hard to start from seed.

Top Secret Tip: The leaves look a lot like pine needles, and they smell wonderful. Whether you're cooking or making homemade potpourri, try crushing the leaves to really bring out the smell even more. If you are starting from seed, more is better. The rosemary seeds don't have a high percent of success when it comes to germination, so plant even more than you normally would: eventually, you'll get one to take hold!

Fun Fact: Some think rosemary helps improve concentration. So the next time you need to do some homework, try smelling a little rosemary. It might make you do better!

Cilantro

Difficulty:

The Basics: Annual, 18 to 24 inches tall

Grow It: Plant seeds with roughly ¼ inch of soil on top. Once you have small sprouts, thin out about 3 to 4 inches apart to avoid crowding. Cilantro doesn't like hot weather, so let it get some sun in the morning or afternoon, but not all day.

Top Secret Tip: To get your seeds (the seeds of cilantro are called coriander) to germinate, gently rub them together and then soak in water for 2 days.

Fun Fact: Some people love the smell of cilantro and compare it to a citrus scent. Others think it's horrible and have compared it to the smell of bug repellent!

Parsley

Difficulty:

The Basics: Annual, 15 to 18 inches tall

Grow It: Some people call it America's favorite herb. Parsley is quick, fun, and fairly easy to grow. Plus, you can use it in almost anything to add a little flavor. The two main types of parsley are flat leaf or curly leaf. Grow it in full sun. It will mature in 40 to 60 days.

Top Secret Tip: Though most people grow parsley as an annual, if you can establish it in your garden, it will come back year after year.

Fun Fact: Parsley is considered a natural breath freshener. And it has almost three times the calcium of an orange! So go ahead and munch away!

Basil

Difficulty: 🥄

The Basics: Annual, 12 to 18 inches tall

Grow It: You'll find many different varieties of basil to plant, including sweet basil, lime basil, Greek basil and more. For most, you can plant seeds inside during winter or outside after the danger of frost has past. Plant leaves are ready to harvest 60 to 90 days after you plant them, but you can start snipping off smaller leaves as soon as they appear. Make sure you have plants in a sunny location that gets 6 to 8 hours of sunlight per day.

Top Secret Tip: Once they've sprouted, thin out plants 6 to 12 inches apart. Then water deeply every 7 to 10 days.

Fun Fact: Basil is another herb that people think has healing powers! People in Haiti think it helps protect them from evil spirits. Some people use basil to help cure warts.

Oregano

Difficulty: 🥄🥄

The Basics: Perennial, Zones 5 to 10, 18 to 24 inches tall

Grow It: Mmmm, oregano! This favorite Italian herb is used in so many dishes. You can plant it directly in your garden in spring and it'll come back year after year. Or grow it indoors in full sun. You can harvest it after 90 or so days.

Top Secret Tip: To get a nice, healthy plant, pinch back your oregano leaves around 6 weeks after you've planted them. This just means you pinch the tips of the leaves before flowers can develop. This will help them grow big and strong.

Fun Fact: Oregano has a reputation for calming nerves and getting rid of sea sickness.

Drying Herbs

Fresh herbs are great for cooking, but you're likely to grow more than you can use while fresh. If you dry some of your herbs, you'll be able to enjoy them for months longer. Here are a few quick tips:

- Pick herbs to dry when the plants are showing little buds, but just before the flowers open. This will give your dried herbs the best flavor.
- You can dry herbs in a dehydrator if you have one. Check your dehydrator's manual for specific directions.
- To dry indoors, simply cut a large bunch of herbs, tie them with a string, and hang them upside down.
- It's better not to dry herbs in direct sun or outside because they often lose their flavor.
- Once herbs are crispy and crumble a little to the touch, they are ready for you to package up and store.
- The best way to store herbs is in a small glass jar. Generally, you should replace your dried herb supply at least every year.

PLANT IT: Soup's On Herb Garden Plan

These herbs add flavor to your favorite soups. Harvest directly from your herb garden for the best flavor. A little bit goes a long way with herbs. Start off with only a few plants each of two to three herbs. You can always add more. Herbs work well in containers. The most important thing is to make sure they get enough light. And consider mixing and matching, based on the flavors you like most.

Difficulty:

Plants: Oregano, rosemary, basil

The Basics: You can buy herb seeds at your local garden center or if you're looking for a jump start, buy plants instead. They are relatively inexpensive, and you can even split the plants with a friend to get more bang for your buck.

Oregano: Oregano is great in tomato-based dishes, especially anything Italian. It's also good with eggs and meats.

Rosemary: Rosemary is good in almost anything it touches, from soups, eggs, and fish to fruits and veggies.

Basil: Use a little basil in your veggie soup and save a little to make your own herb-based vinegar for salad dressing, too.

Growing Bay Leaves

Dozens of recipes call for bay leaves. Who knew such a little bitty leaf could pack such a punch? Just one in a slow cooker all day adds amazing flavor to your favorite dish. It's not a typical herb, though. These small, powerful leaves grow on evergreen-like trees that can get up to forty feet tall! You can have your own bay tree. Check with your local nursery to see if they can help you get one. Or go online to find one. When bay trees are in pots, they rarely grow more than six feet. Keep it in a sunny area year-round, outside in summer and inside in winter. Pretty soon, everyone you know will be coming to you for homegrown bay leaves!

Oregano

Rosemary

Basil

eat IT: Lovely Lemons

Lemons are a great fruit choice in winter: they are in season year-round and remind you that lemonade-drinking days aren't far away. They have a reputation for being sour, but they can be sweet, too! All you need is the right recipe. Whether you're buying lemons from the store or are growing your own, it's a great time to enjoy this citrus treat.

Lemonade Cupcakes

Difficulty:

Yield: 24 cupcakes

12 ounces frozen lemonade concentrate

½ cup fresh lemon juice

1 package white cake mix

8 ounces sour cream

3 ounces cream cheese

3 large eggs

1 can vanilla frosting

1 Preheat oven to 350°F.

2 Combine lemonade concentrate, lemon juice, cake mix, sour cream, cream cheese, and eggs in a large bowl.

3 Beat for 4 minutes.

4 Spoon batter into muffin tins lined with paper baking cups.

5 Bake for 22 minutes. Cool completely and frost.

Yummy Lemon Bars

Difficulty: 🍴🍴

Yield: 24 servings (2-inch squares)

Crust:

Nonstick cooking spray

2 cups flour

1 cup confectioner's sugar

¾ teaspoon salt

1½ sticks butter (12 tablespoons)

Filling:

4 eggs

1½ cups granulated sugar

5 tablespoons flour

1½ teaspoons lemon zest

⅔ cup lemon juice

¼ cup milk

½ teaspoon salt

Confectioner's sugar for topping

1 Heat the oven to 350°F.

2 Spray a 9" × 13" pan with nonstick cooking spray.

3 Make the crust by combining flour, confectioner's sugar and salt in bowl.

4 Cut in butter to make a crumbly mixture.

5 Press the crust mixture into the prepared pan (if your fingers get too sticky, dip them into flour).

6 Bake for 20 minutes.

7 While the crust is cooking prepare the filling. Mix eggs, granulated sugar, flour, lemon zest, lemon juice, milk, and salt in bowl.

8 Pour filling mixture over baked crust.

9 Lower oven temperature to 325°F and bake for 25 minutes longer or until filling is set (not jiggling).

10 Sprinkle with confectioner's sugar when bars are completely cooled.

Lemon Snow Ice Cream

Difficulty:

Yield: 8 servings

8 cups fresh snow or shaved ice

½ cup white sugar

1 cup milk

¼ cup lemon juice

1 Mix fresh snow or shaved ice, sugar, milk, and lemon juice together in large bowl.

2 Eat immediately!

Growing Lemons

Did you know that you can grow lemons indoors? You might need a little patience, because it can take a little while for an indoor lemon tree to get established. But it's a great way to keep on gardening, even in winter. Here are a few tips to keep your lemons growing strong:

- Lemon trees do best in temperatures that average 70 degrees during the day and 55 degrees during night.
- They love light, so make sure you have yours set up near a sunny window.
- During warm periods, put your lemon tree outside.
- Keep your lemon tree in a large 3-gallon pot (or a container recommended on the plant label) so that it's easy to move in and out.
- Be patient! It may take several months, a year, or sometimes more to finally see your first lemon, but it's worth the wait. And in the meantime, it's an easy-to-care-for houseplant.

 RECYCLE IT:
Seed Catalog Art

January is unofficially seed catalog month. Most gardeners can't grow outside during this time, but that doesn't stop them from dreaming! Seed catalogs are a great way to see what's new in the gardening world, and they certainly do cheer you up in midwinter! Sign up for as many as you can to enjoy the pictures and inspiration. Once you've gone through them all, there are lots of ways to keep enjoying them. Flower bookmarks give your books a touch of spring, and making Valentine's Day cards can give you a head start on next month's to-do list. Decoupage flower frames are the perfect gift for someone who needs a touch of color in their life, and custom garden plans will help work out your spring fever—and keep your garden plans on track.

Flower Bookmarks

Difficulty:

Materials:

- Sturdy poster board or a thin piece of cardboard (like a cereal box)
- Seed catalogs
- Your preferred adhesive—a glue stick, craft glue, or paste

1   Cut poster board or cardboard into bookmark-sized rectangles.

2   Go through your seed catalogs, find your favorite flowers and plants, and cut out their pictures. It might be fun to make themed bookmarks. For instance, you could choose all pink flowers or all roses.

3   Attach the photos to the bookmark bases with glue or paste. (A glue stick is a great option for this because it won't wrinkle the paper.) You can either paste a single photo on each or several, depending on what you like. Smooth it out and let dry.

Valentine Cards

Difficulty:

Materials:

- ☐ Construction paper
- ☐ Seed catalogs
- ☐ Your preferred adhesive—a glue stick, craft glue, or paste
- ☐ Something to write with—such as pencils, crayons, or markers

1 Start by folding the construction paper to make a card shape.

2 Next, cut out your favorite flowers from your seed catalogs and glue or paste into place.

3 Add a sweet saying, like "Our friendship is blooming," "We are best buds," or "Let's grow together, Valentine."

Custom Garden Plan

Difficulty:

Materials

- ☐ Seed catalogs
- ☐ Something to draw on—like poster board, recycled cardboard, or paper
- ☐ Something to write with—like pencils, crayons, or markers
- ☐ Your preferred adhesive—a glue stick, craft glue, or paste

1 Cut out pictures of any plants you already have in your garden from the seed catalogs. Then go through the catalogs again, and cut all the plants you want to add.

2 Draw a large diagram of your garden on poster board, recycled cardboard, or paper. Start gluing on the plants that you already have planted outside. Then add the new ones you want to grow this year.

3 Hang up your plan so that it's a constant reminder that spring is just around the corner! It will also help you make a list of plants you need to order or buy to complete your garden.

Flower Frame

Difficulty:

1 Start off by cutting out dozens of flower pictures from the seed catalog.

2 Remove any glass or plastic from inside the frame, as well as the backing.

3 Arrange the pictures on the face of the frame, overlapping as much as you like to create a mosaic look.

4 Carefully glue the bottom layer of pictures to the frame section by section. Really cover the frame with glue before you put the pictures down, and be careful to gently smooth out any creases or wrinkles. Use your glue spreader if you need to. Let the first layer dry.

5 Add another layer of craft glue and carefully paste any pictures that will form the second layer. Let this layer dry. Repeat this step until all of your pictures are glued down.

6 Once the layer of pictures is dry, add one final generous coat of glue to the top. Use your glue smoother to keep it from streaking, pooling, or bubbling. You can add several layers of glue if you like, drying between each one.

7 Finally, when the top layer of glue is dry, put the frame back together and enjoy your final piece!

Make It: Awesome Aromas

Making candles is a great activity to get rid of the winter blues. Pick up a candle kit at your local craft store or just gather up these supplies.

Do-It-Yourself Herb Candles

Difficulty:

Materials
- [ ] Wax
- [ ] Pan
- [ ] Wick
- [ ] Candle container (or recycle a jar)
- [ ] Herbs
- [ ] Fragrance
- [ ] Candle coloring

1 First off, choose your wax. There are many options including beeswax, soy wax, palm wax, and gel wax. (Paraffin is also an option.) Don't worry about choosing the perfect wax: they're all fairly easy to work with. Find one that meets your budget and give it a try.

2 Read the instructions on your wax of choice. Generally, you will heat your wax in a pan over the stove. Keep it on a low heat so it doesn't burn. Stay close to the melting wax and stir it gently.

3 Just before your wax is completely melted, place your wick into your candle mold. You might have to move it around a bit to get it in just the right position.

4 Prior to the wax melting, crush your herbs of choice so that they are in small pieces.

5 Once the wax is melted, add herbs, fragrance, and/or special coloring. Stir.

6 Gently pour the mixture into your candle container, making sure your wick doesn't move out of place. You might have to hold it in place until the candle starts to harden a bit.

7 Once it hardens, use the remaining herbs to decorate the top of the candle. Press the herbs into the outside while it's still soft. This will add fragrance and give the candle a natural look overall.

Fun with Gel

Gel is a great medium for candles if you want to suspend objects in your candle for a decorative touch. For example, leaving your herbs in large chunks is perfect for gel wax. Though these candles are better for display than burning, it adds great visual interest and makes it easy to personalize the candle if you're giving it away as a gift. Here are some other fun items to try placing in gel wax candles:

- Peppermints
- Small fake flowers
- Cinnamon sticks
- Dice
- Marbles
- Screws
- Rice

✂ Make it: Plant Markers Made Easy

It's never too early to start working on some garden projects. Plant markers are a fun indoor activity. You can often find things around your house to recycle into plant markers—like the paint-stirring sticks you get at the hardware store! You can also use old tin cans, rocks, scrap wood, or adorable (and inexpensive) miniature flowerpots. Take a look around to see what else you might be able to convert.

Popsicle Sticks

Difficulty:

Materials
- ☐ Popsicle sticks
- ☐ Crayons and markers

1 Decorate your clean, dry Popsicle sticks with crayons and markers.

2 When you're ready, just add a plant name to each one!

Paint Sticks

Difficulty:

Materials

- Paint-stirring sticks—the kind you get from the hardware store
- Strong scissors (optional)
- Permanent marker
- Fun decorations—such as pictures from a seed catalog, paint, and colored markers

1 Gather your paint-stirring sticks. If you want your supplies to last longer, cut in half using a strong pair of scissors.

2 If you already know what you're planting in the spring, write your plant names on the stirring sticks in permanent marker.

3 If you're not sure what you'll be growing, use whatever decorations you've chosen to spruce up the plain wood.

Veggie Cans

Difficulty:

Materials

- Empty tin cans
- Markers
- Glue
- Fun decorations that will last outdoors—like buttons

1 To prep the cans, remove the outside wrapper, clean them, and then set out to dry. Decorate the cans using markers or glue on old buttons.

2 If you know what plant each can will mark, make sure to write the names clearly.

Rocks

Difficulty:

Materials

- Rocks big enough to write on clearly
- Paint, markers, and decorations

1 Make sure your rocks are clean and dry.

2 Dress up the rocks and write or paint your plant names on each one.

Scrap Wood

Difficulty:

Materials

- ☐ Scrap wood of all sizes
- ☐ Hammer and nails *or* wood glue
- ☐ Something to cut wood—if you need it
- ☐ Paint or markers

1 Pair pieces of wood in T shapes—one to go into the ground and one to display the plant name. If your scraps are big, cut them to size if you need to, but don't worry too much about each one being the same size—it'll be fun to have them all be different.

2 When you've decided how each pair will look together, secure them with nails or glue.

3 Decorate each one and write plant names with paint or markers.

Miniature Flowerpots

Difficulty:

Materials

- ☐ Miniature flowerpots
- ☐ Paint (optional)
- ☐ Modeling clay, like Play-Doh
- ☐ Bolts that fit through the pot's drainage hole or old forks and spoons that can spend a season outside, one for each pot you'll make

1 Paint the pots, if you wish, adding a name of a plant you know you'll grow next to each one. (Be careful to make sure that the names are *right-side up*, depending on how you are going to position your plant markers; double-check step 3 to make sure. You want to be able to read what you wrote!)

2 When the pots dry, fill each with the modeling clay.

3 If you're using bolts, turn the pot right side up and insert the bolt into the modeling clay. (The example pictured shows a bolt and the pot right side up.) If you're using old silverware, insert the tines of a fork or the bowl of a spoon into the modeling clay.

4 Let modeling clay dry overnight. In the spring, you'll push the bottom of the bolt or handle-end into the ground to display your new plant markers!

FEBRUARY

GR🌱W IT: Plants

All of these plants are considered spring bulbs. You'll plant most of your bulbs in fall, but you'll start to see them peek through the ground in February. The little green spikes are a welcome sight because it means that spring is just around the corner. If your bulbs start to emerge and then it snows again, just cover them up with a cardboard box to help protect them.

Allium

Difficulty:

The Basics: Perennial, Zones 4 to 8, 20 to 30 inches tall

Grow It: Alliums are like a magic wand with a giant colorful ball sitting on top. Plant them in the fall, about 8 to 10 inches deep and in a sunny spot. Most alliums have pink or purple blooms, but you can also find some that are bluish in color.

Top Secret Tip: Alliums bloom in late spring, after daffodils but before lots of summer flowers. So they are great for that in-between time.

Fun Fact: Alliums are really part of the onion family. Take a sniff or just pinch off part of a leaf to see if you can smell it.

Snowdrop

Difficulty:

The Basics: Perennial, Zones 4 to 7, 4 to 10 inches tall

Grow It: These plants get their name because the white flowers look like a drop of white snow, hanging in the air. They are one of the earliest plants to bloom in spring. Plant in fall before the first frost. They need a cold period over winter to bloom in spring. If you live in a warmer area, you might get these to bloom year-round.

Top Secret Tip: More is better with these flowers. The blooms are small, so plant them in bunches for a fuller look.

Fun Fact: Snowdrops will even pop out and bloom when there's still snow on the ground!

Crocus

Difficulty:

The Basics: Perennial, Zones 4 to 8, 4 to 6 inches tall

Grow It: Plant several of these in fall a few inches deep and a few inches apart. You can also find fall-blooming crocuses to plant in late spring. These blooms might be small, but they can make a big, colorful impact.

Top Secret Tip: Try planting a few crocus bulbs directly into your lawn. Its small blooms look beautiful as it pops up close to the ground.

Fun Fact: You can cook with some crocus varieties (like crocus sativus), but most others are poisonous if you eat it, so be careful!

Iris

Difficulty:

The Basics: Perennial, Zones 4 to 8, up to 3 feet tall

Grow It: Irises don't actually come from bulbs like a lot of other early bloomers. Instead they sprout from rhizomes. (Rhizomes are just a type of root, but it's bigger and thicker.) Plant them in late summer in full sunshine and then they'll be ready to bloom the following spring. You can also find irises to plant in early spring after the ground is thawed.

Top Secret Tip: Find the right iris for you before you plant it. Varieties include the bearded iris that blooms in May (it kind of looks like it has a beard) and the Siberian iris, which you'll find growing in the wild in summer.

Fun Fact: This flower was named after Iris, the Greek goddess of the rainbow.

Hyacinth

Difficulty:

The Basics: Perennial, Zones 4 to 8, 8 to 10 inches tall

Grow It: Plant hyacinths in the fall, a few weeks before the ground freezes. The tall stalks will do okay in some shade, but hyacinths really like lots of sun. Once it blooms, let it finish growing and cut down the stems for summer. This will keep it healthy for years to come.

Top Secret Tip: If you like color, hyacinth is the spring bulb for you. You can find it in pink, purple, yellow, white and more. Or try mixing them all up, too.

Fun Fact: March 7 is considered World Hyacinth Day.

Plant Now for Summer

While the flowers here are all ones you plant in fall to bloom in spring, there are some others you can plant *now* for summer blossoms. Look for these at your local plant store. Then you'll have great color this summer.

- Caladium
- Cana lily
- Dahlias
- Gladiolus
- Nerine

PLANT IT:
Heart Garden Plan

It's the month of love, so what better way to celebrate than with a few heart-shaped plants? You can find most of these in early spring, depending on when the danger of frost passes in your area. These will also all do great in a shady spot, so plant away for yourself or your sweetheart.

Difficulty:

Plants: Hosta, caladium, bleeding heart

The Basics: Use one hosta, three caladiums and two bleeding hearts, positioning the hosta in the middle and the bleeding hearts to spill over the edges. A large 3-gallon pot will work well. For all containers, use a special container soil mix. If you plant in early spring when it's still cold out, be sure to bring your container inside when it gets cold.

Hosta: Many hostas already have heart-shaped blooms, but specifically look for ones with "heart" in the name, like Heart's Content, Cheatin' Heart, and Heartsong.

Caladium: It has beautiful colors such as red and pink. They always make shady spots a little brighter.

Bleeding heart: Its tiny pink spring blooms look just like its name says—like a heart that is bleeding. Even after the blooms fade, it still gives good green foliage.

A Little Heart

Lots of leaves have heart shapes. Here's a look at some of the most common. Go on a leaf hunt and see if you can find others.

- Lilac
- Redbud
- Clovers
- Elephant ear

Hosta

Caladium

Bleeding Heart

Radishes are an easy veggie to grow. They do best in cooler temperatures, so depending on where you live, plant in February or March. It's appropriate that radishes are the featured veggie for February, too. They look a lot like hearts.

Tortilla Radish Rolls

Difficulty:

Yield: 48 servings

8-ounce package cream cheese, softened

1 package powdered dressing mix

½ cup chopped radishes

1 4-ounce can chopped green chilies

8 large flour tortillas

1½ pounds thinly sliced meat of choice (turkey, roast beef, ham, etc.)

1   Mix cream cheese, dressing mix, radishes, and green chilies together.

2   Divide and spread the mix evenly onto the eight tortillas.

3   Cover with the meat slices.

4   Roll the tortillas tightly, and chill for 2 hours.

5   Cut off the roll ends, and make into 1-inch slices and arrange on a plate or tray.

Black Bean and Radish Soup

Difficulty:

Yield: 8 servings

1 cup chopped radishes

Juice of one lemon

½ teaspoon salt

1 teaspoon onion powder

½ teaspoon garlic powder

4 cups cooked black beans

2 cups water

Sour cream, diced cilantro and shredded cheese for garnish

1 Blend radishes, lemon juice, salt, onion powder, and garlic powder with 1 cup of beans. Mash together with a fork until it has a slightly chunky texture.

2 Add mixture to additional 3 cups of black beans and water in medium pot. If soup is too thick, add more water.

3 Cook on low heat for 20 to 30 minutes, serve with a little sour cream, diced cilantro, and cheese on top.

Broccoli Radish Skillet

Difficulty:

Yield: 6 servings

1 teaspoon olive oil

4 cups broccoli florets

2 cups chopped radishes

1 envelope powdered onion soup mix

1½ cups water

1 Heat oil in pan over medium heat. Cook broccoli and radishes in pan for about 2 minutes.

2 Mix soup and water in medium bowl, then stir into pan. Bring to a boil over high heat.

3 Reduce heat to medium low and simmer about 6 minutes or until broccoli is tender.

Radish Chips

Difficulty:

Yield: 6 servings

½ cup garlic-flavored olive oil

2 cups radishes, cut in thin slices

Salt to taste

Ranch dressing to dip

1 Heat olive oil in nonstick pan on medium heat.

2 Add the radishes to the oil. Sauté until edges start to wrinkle up a bit.

3 Drain the olive oil, place radishes on a paper towel, and salt to taste.

4 You can also try dipping them in a ranch sauce.

Tips for Growing Radishes

- Radishes are one of the fastest-growing vegetables. Plant them in spring, and you'll get results in less than 30 days!
- You don't need a lot of space to grow radishes. They'll grow almost anywhere, including a container.
- Plant seeds directly into the ground as early as you can in spring. Once the sprouts emerge, thin so they are about 1 to 2 inches apart.
- Radishes are root veggies, so you'll pull them up out of the ground when it's time to harvest. Don't let them get too big. They taste better when they are smaller. (If they've cracked, that's too big.)
- Some radishes are hotter in flavor, while others are sweeter. Look around for a few varieties to try.

♻ RECYCLE IT: Food for Birds

February is National Bird-Feeding Month, and birds like cardinals, chickadees, and juncos will be stopping by backyard feeders for seed. You don't have to buy an expensive feeder when you can easily make your own instead. This one is made from all recycled items.

Basket of Birdseed

Difficulty: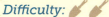

Materials

- ☐ Basket
- ☐ Plate, preferably something that will hold up to the weather
- ☐ Decorations, check out the list in the sidebar for inspiration
- ☐ Birdseed

1 Clean up your basket and make sure it's sturdy. You'll be putting a plate inside it, so you'll want to make sure it's not likely to break.

2 Securely nest your plate inside your basket. (If you're at a loss for supplies that you can recycle, you can always check your local thrift store.)

3 Dress up your basket a bit. Wooden beads and an inviting sign make for a pretty picture. You can do just about anything to match your garden themes. Just use your imagination.

4 Hang up your feeder, then pour birdseed on top of the plate. (If there's enough room in your basket, you can also store extra seed underneath the plate in a plastic bag.)

Dress It Up!

Whether you make your own bird feeder or buy one from a store, you can always dress it up. Here are a few ideas of things to add to your feeder.

- Buttons
- Beads
- Ribbon
- Stickers
- Magnets

♻ RECYCLE IT:
Water for the Birds

Not all birds eat bird seed, but all birds do drink water! And butterflies and other insects will stop by for water, too! Birdbaths are nice, but they can be a little pricey. It's not hard to offer water, though. You can use a simple bowl, but these recycled projects are great ways to give new purpose to otherwise dreary items.

Wastebasket Birdbath

Difficulty:

Materials

- ☐ Old wastebasket
- ☐ Shallow bowl that fits well on top of the wastebasket
- ☐ Decorations
- ☐ Glue

1 Clean up the wastebasket inside and out. It should be rather small—something you might find in a bathroom.

2 Place the shallow bowl on top so it fits snugly.

3 Now it's time to decorate! Here, buttons were carefully attached to the outside of the wastebasket with hot glue. Then letter stickers were added to the top. Pick your own outdoorsy look to get your garden going.

4 Pick a good spot for your birdbath and add water.

Kitchen Faucet Birdbath

Difficulty:

Materials

- Kitchen faucet
- Large, sturdy paperclip
- Pliers
- Pie pan
- Nail
- Fishing wire
- Beads
- Screws and screwdriver
- Drill and bits (optional)

1. Bend half of the paperclip around the faucet spout. Twist the other half into a hook that hangs downward. You'll be hanging your birdbath from this paperclip hook, so make sure it's sturdy. Pliers will help you get the job done quickly.

2. Next, punch three to four holes around the edges of the pie pan using a nail. Space them as evenly as possible so your birdbath can hang squarely.

3. Tie fishing wire through the holes and around the edge of the pie pan. Make sure each length of wire is the same length—about 7 to 8 inches—so the pie pan hangs evenly.

4. If you'd like, add beads to the wire as decoration.

5. Gather the wire together above the pie pan to make sure the pan is level when it hangs. Make any adjustments you need. Tie the wire together in a knot at the top, leaving a loop sturdy enough to hold the pie pan when you hang it. Attach the top loop to the paperclip hook on the spout.

6. Finally, set up your faucet birdbath outside. You can use screws to attach it to the top of a fence or the top of a tree branch so it looks like your faucet is sprouting from the surface. If there aren't holes already in the base of the faucet, you'll need to drill a couple.

If you don't have an old faucet lying around the house, talk to your local plumber or handyman. They have lots of faucets and would probably be happy to give you one to recycle.

Early spring is the perfect time to get your birdhouses out. Traditional wooden birdhouses made of wood are sturdy, will last for several seasons and are a favorite among birds. But here is a less-than-traditional idea that is free to make and still offers a great home for your backyard visitors.

Sturdier-Than-It-Looks String Birdhouse

Difficulty:

Materials

- ☐ String, twine, or yarn (60 feet or more)
- ☐ Bowl
- ☐ Glue (1–2 cups)
- ☐ Food coloring (optional)
- ☐ Rubber gloves (optional)
- ☐ Latex balloon

1 Make sure the string is sturdy and will hold up well over time. Cut string into 20 3–foot long pieces. If you use colorful sting, you won't need the food coloring—skip to Step 3.

2 Mix glue and dye in bowl until you like the color. Wear rubber gloves to protect your hands from the mess while you're handling the dye-and-glue mix.

3 Soak string in glue for a half hour, covering each piece.

4 While the string is soaking, blow up the latex balloon (not *too* big) and attach it to your workspace.

5 Take string out a few pieces at a time. Wrap the string around the balloon until every bit is covered except for a small opening where birds will fly in and out.

6 Hang the balloon to dry for 24 to 48 hours total.

7 If the balloon pops while the birdhouse is drying, simply remove it and blow up another balloon inside the string. This is really important. You don't want the shape to collapse before it's dry, so keep an eye on it.

8 Once dry, pop the balloon and remove it. Then hang outside for the birds. It's plenty sturdy to last a season. And you might even get two seasons out of it. To give it a little extra support, spray with a waterproof latex.

The "Hole" Truth

Did you know that most people make their birdhouse holes too big? If the entrance into a birdhouse is too big, birds won't use it because predators like snakes and raccoons can reach inside. Different birds prefer different size entrance holes, so look online for advice on how big you need to make the hole for the birds you'd like to attract. Start off small. You can always make a hole bigger, but it's pretty hard to make one smaller!

Common Birdhouse Entry Sizes	
Backyard Birds	**Size of Birdhouse Entry Used**
Tufted titmouse, chickadee, nuthatch, downy woodpecker	1¼ inches
Eastern bluebird, tree swallow	1½ inches
Purple martin, northern flicker	2½ inches
House wren	1⅛ inches
Redheaded woodpecker	2 inches

More Untraditional Birdhouse Ideas

1. **Soccer ball.** If you have one with a leak, don't throw it out! Instead, turn it into a birdhouse. Just cut a small hole and it'll make a perfect home.
2. **Cardboard.** It's not going to hold up for more than a season, but you can still make a birdhouse out of cardboard. Use two layers of cardboard to make it sturdier, and hang in a well-protected area so it doesn't get torn up.
3. **Tupperware.** Find an old plastic container that has a lid. Decorate the outside and secure the lid tight. Then make a hole in the side and hang.

MARCH

GR🌱W IT: Plants

By March, it's time to think about planting spring-blooming trees and shrubs. They will take up more room in your garden than bulbs or bunches of flowers, but they have some of the prettiest springtime blooms around. Pick a couple of these to add to your backyard this spring. Before long, you'll have gorgeous spring color as early as March!

Redbud

Difficulty: 🌱🌱

The Basics: Perennial, Zones 4 to 9, up to 20 to 30 feet tall

Grow It: Redbuds are one of the earliest blooming trees. A lot of times, when there are no other leaves on the trees, redbud is shining bright with its bright reddish purple flowers. You can grow redbud in a mix of sun and shade and in many different kinds of soil, so it's a great tree for almost every backyard.

Top Secret Tip: Don't overwater redbud. It actually does pretty well in dry areas and doesn't like spots that are too wet. Careful and correct pruning will help strengthen this tree.

Fun Fact: Redbuds have a reputation for having weak wood, so don't go using it for a climbing tree!

Lilac

Difficulty: 🌱🌱

The Basics: Perennial, Zones 3 to 8, up to 10 feet tall

Grow It: Lilacs are one of the best-smelling shrubs you can grow. They smell wonderful when they bloom in late spring. They also have gorgeous bluish-purple blooms! Grow in full sun.

Top Secret Tip: Lilacs need good drainage. If you have a little hill on which to plant them, it can really help your lilacs stay healthy over the long term.

Fun Fact: American presidents have a history of growing lilacs, including George Washington and Thomas Jefferson.

Forsythia

Difficulty: 🌱🌱

The Basics: Perennial, Zones 4 to 8, up to 5 feet tall

Grow It: Forsythia is like sunshine on a rainy day. The flowers on this shrub are nearly as bright as the sun and look beautiful in early to mid-spring. They like full sun but will do well in some shade, too. Some forsythias are only a few feet tall but several feet wide. Find one to fit your space; there are many different varieties available. Ask your local garden center.

Top Secret Tip: Lots of shrubs can take years to bloom, but forsythia is a fast grower! If you want quick results, forsythia is a really good choice.

Fun Fact: Sometimes you can force these to bloom indoors. Cut a branch and give it a try over the winter.

Azalea

Difficulty:

The Basics: Perennial, Zones 5 to 8, up to 8 feet tall

Grow It: You can find dozens and dozens of azalea choices out there. Some do better in colder areas than others. You can also find some that grow short and others that will end up tall. The best thing to do is to ask around at your nearby garden center. They'll carry good varieties that will do well in your area. Grow in full sun to partial shade.

Top Secret Tip: Azaleas do best in spots that receive some morning sun but are a bit shady during the hottest part of the day.

Fun Fact: Some people call azaleas "rhododendrons." They are almost the same plant, growing well in the same conditions. Now you'll have even more choices to pick from.

Peonies

Difficulty:

The Basics: Perennial, Zones 3 to 9, up to 4 feet tall

Grow It: Peonies have huge, beautiful blooms. They also smell great and are pretty easy to grow. They do best in full sun to partial shade. You can find peonies in almost every color imaginable. They often have fun names, like "Raspberry Sundae."

Top Secret Tip: Most peonies have so many large blooms that they droop down to the ground and break the stems. Pick these to put in water or give away. Peony blooms are short-lived anyway, so you might as well enjoy them *and* take some weight away from your shrubs.

Fun Fact: Some clumps of peonies can live 50 years or more!

Tips for Planting Shrubs and Trees

- Look for an overall good, healthy plant when choosing a tree or shrub. Size is not the most important thing to look for. Instead, focus on finding ones that have healthy stems and bark (without rips or tears).
- Plant trees and shrubs either in fall after they are considered dormant or in early spring before they have started to bloom.
- Make sure you have good drainage.
- You must give your tree or shrub plenty of room to grow. Dig a hole twice the width of and at least 6 inches deeper than your plant's roots or root-ball.
- Be sure to give your trees and shrubs plenty of water early on to help them get established.

PLANT IT: Purple in Springtime Plan

If you like purple, then you'll love this combination! These don't all bloom at the same time, so you'll have a garden of purple for several weeks in a row.

Difficulty:

Plants: Lilac, iris, crocus

The Basics: When pairing up plants, the most important thing to remember is to look at light needs. Lilacs, irises, and crocuses all do great in full sun, so this makes them great companions. You might have to do a little planning ahead for planting these (plant in summer and fall). If you plant one lilac, 10 to 12 irises and another 10 to 12 crocuses, you'll need about a 5-foot square space.

Lilac: The purple blooms are beautiful. They will make a great backdrop to the other purple blooms you grow. Plant this shrub in full sun in an area where you can enjoy its sweet smell.

Iris: If you can time it right, your lilacs and irises could bloom at the same time. They'll look great together because lilacs are lighter in color and irises are darker. Irises do best in full sun. Don't forget to plant in summer or late fall for late spring blooms.

Crocus: They are one of the earliest spring flowers, so they'll be blooming long before lilacs and irises, but they'll definitely get you into the purple spirit. Make sure to specifically plant purple varieties such as Whitewell Purple crocus. (Purple is a popular crocus option, so check your local garden center.)

Lilac

Iris

Crocus

eat it:
Powerhouse Potatoes

Potatoes are fun to grow, and you can make so many different dishes with them. Here are a few recipes to try with your own fresh potatoes from the garden.

Country Mashed Potatoes

Difficulty:

Yield: 8 servings

5 to 7 large potatoes

1 stick butter

¾ to 1 cup of half-and-half

2 teaspoons salt

1 teaspoon pepper

1　Cut potatoes into 1-inch square chunks. Place in large pot, cover with water, and boil until potatoes are tender.

2　Drain water off potatoes and place them into mixing bowl with butter.

3　When butter has softened, begin to mix with beaters or stand mixer.

4　Beat the potatoes until smooth and add half-and-half gradually. The potatoes should be fluffy and just a little on the thin side because they will continue to firm up as they sit.

5　Add salt and pepper to taste.

Slow Cooker Scalloped Potatoes

Difficulty:

Yield: 8 servings

3 pounds potatoes, peeled and thinly sliced

1 cup shredded Cheddar cheese

1 cup diced, cooked ham

1 cup cream of chicken soup from concentrate

½ cup water

1 teaspoon garlic powder

1 teaspoon salt

1 teaspoon black pepper

1 Place sliced potatoes, shredded cheese, and ham in slow cooker. Mix to evenly distribute ingredients.

2 Mix together soup and water in medium bowl. Season to taste with garlic powder, salt, and pepper.

3 Pour seasoned soup evenly over the potatoes in slow cooker.

4 Cover and cook on high for 4 hours.

Potato Casserole

Difficulty:

Yield: 8 servings

10 to 12 potatoes

1 pound ground beef, browned

2 cans cream of chicken soup from concentrate

Salt and pepper to taste

1 cup Cheddar cheese

1 Preheat oven to 350°F.

2 Slice potatoes in rounds, place in large pot, cover with water, and boil until cooked.

3 Mix browned ground beef and cream of chicken soup.

4 Salt and pepper to taste.

5 Layer meat, potatoes, and cheese until 9" × 13" pan is full.

6 Bake for 30 minutes.

Potato Salad

Difficulty:

Yield: 8 servings

4 cups cooked chunked or mashed potatoes

6 to 8 boiled eggs, chopped

½ cup sweet relish

½ cup onions, chopped

⅓ cup mayonnaise

1 tablespoon mustard

½ teaspoon salt

½ teaspoon pepper

1 Mix all ingredients together in large bowl. All ingredients may be increased or reduced according to taste.

2 If you use leftover mashed potatoes, you should reduce or omit salt and pepper, since they may have already been added.

3 Can be served warm or chilled.

4 Refrigerate leftovers up to 3 days.

Tips for Growing Potatoes

- Potatoes need full sun, and they do best in loose soil.
- Potatoes are susceptible to disease, so make sure you buy good-quality planting potatoes from a good source.
- Plant potatoes in the soil as soon as you can dig into the ground in spring (once it's not frozen anymore!). If frost comes, you do need to protect your potato plants.
- When you plant potatoes, you don't use typical "seeds" like with most veggies. Planting potatoes look like regular potatoes. You simply cut them up into different potato "eyes" and plant in the ground with the eye pointing up.
- Potatoes are tubers, which means they grow downward into the ground while sending a green plant above the ground.
- Since you can't see them growing, it's a little tricky to know when to harvest. Check the harvest date on the specific variety of potatoes you choose and be sure to time it.
- Potatoes can be tricky to grow, so be sure to read the directions on your specific variety. And if you decide to skip growing potatoes, your local farmers' market will have plenty to choose from!

♻ RECYCLE IT: Seed Starting

Depending on where you live, March is a great time for seed starting. If you start seeds much earlier than this, chances are they'll die before it's warm enough to plant them outside. You don't need a lot of expensive seed-starting equipment, either: you can make your own! Here are a few money-saving ideas to start seeds with materials from around your house!

Seed Roll-Ups

Difficulty:

Materials
- Empty toilet paper or paper towel rolls
- Paper towels
- Potting soil
- Seeds to start

1 Cut toilet paper rolls in half; cut paper towel rolls in thirds. Cover the bottom with a small square of paper towel (a few inches) and secure with tape or glue.

2 Fill rolls about ¾ full with soil.

3 Gently press your seeds (2 to 4 each) into the soil, no more than the depth of your fingernail. Start a new set of seeds in each roll.

4 Water your seeds with about a teaspoon of water and put in a sunny window. It's very important not to water them too much.

5 When you're ready to plant your seeds, just plop the entire roll into the ground. The cardboard is biodegradable and will be fine in your soil.

Mini Greenhouse

Difficulty:

1 Clean out your berry container and fill halfway with soil.

2 Plant seeds in the soil, again pressing them into the soil no more than the depth of your fingernail. Check your seed packets' instructions for how close together you should start them.

3 Place in a sunny area and keep the lid closed for the first few days to help the seeds germinate. Water when your soil is dry to the touch.

4 Once you're ready to plant your seeds, gently scoop them out with a spoon and plant outside.

Seed-Starting Tips

• One of the biggest mistakes people make is not giving their seeds enough light. When this happens, the sprouts get "leggy," meaning they are tall, stringy, and weak. This happens because they are trying to stretch to find light. Consider using a grow light to help get your seeds started. You can buy a 60W grow bulb at your local garden center. Then put it in a lamp.

• Seeds need to be started in a warm location so they can germinate. A grow light will help, but so will a nice, south-facing kitchen window

• Keep your seeds away from your pets! If you have a cat, there's a good chance she will try to munch on the sprouts.

• Make sure you have good drainage. Little seeds don't need much water, and if you don't have good drainage, your soil will be too wet and you won't have good air flow.

• Don't forget to harden off your seedlings. Hardening off means you should gently help your little plants get used to new growing conditions (from the warm, stable conditions of being inside to moving outside where temperatures fluctuate and the spring wind can sometimes blow hard). Take them outside and keep them protected the first day or two before finally planting.

• Finally, sometimes it's best to move the plants outside right away. Don't worry about growing a big plant. If it's smaller but strong (has a strong stem and is a healthy green color), it can do just fine.

MAKE IT:
Seed Planting Made Easy

Seeds mats are an easier way to plant seeds directly into the ground in spring. Seeds are often teeny tiny, very hard to see, and easy to lose track of in a big patch of dark dirt. Also, sprinkling dozens of seeds across a bed—big or small—is wasteful when you only need a few. Seed mats provide the perfect solution. They trap tiny seeds in place so you can just unroll your mat and cover it with soil. These directions are for a spider seed mat that resembles the cleome flowers it will sprout, but you can do this with any seed or shape.

Spider Flower Seed Mat

Difficulty:

Materials
- ☐ Paper towel
- ☐ Scissors
- ☐ Glue
- ☐ Seeds

1 Cut paper towel into the shape you want. To make a spider shape, cut a small circle, a large circle, and eight spider legs.

2 Glue the spider body together and attach the legs.

3 Position seeds onto paper towel mat and gently glue down. Make sure you don't use too much glue: you only need a tiny dab. Also, pay attention to how far apart you are positioning your seeds. You should be following the directions on the back of your seed packet. This is the biggest advantage to using seed mats. You don't have to thin out your seeds later on because they are already perfectly spaced!

4 Once the glue is dry, fold or roll up the mat until it's time to plant outside.

5 Read the instructions on the seed packet to know how much soil and water to sprinkle over your seeds. Then water, watch, and wait.

Veggies in Containers

Gardening in containers is an easy way to grow veggies. It proves that you don't need a lot of space, money, or special equipment! In fact, you can grow your favorite fruits or vegetables right off of your patio, as long as the plants have enough sun. With this idea, you can use old plastic bins, extra containers, buckets, or even an old canvas bag filled with soil.

Veggies in Small Spaces

Difficulty:

Materials

- [ ] Plastic bins, containers, buckets, canvas bags
- [ ] Soil
- [ ] Veggie plants or seeds

1 Make sure the containers you choose aren't too shallow. Many vegetables—such as tomatoes and peppers—should be grown in containers at least 1 foot deep. You can get away with shallower containers when growing smaller plants like radishes or lettuce.

2 Fill containers with a good soil mix (you can find soil mixes specifically devised for veggie gardening).

3 Add plants or seeds and water. If using seeds, be sure to thin out once they've sprouted so that you only have a few plants in each container and so each plant has at least the required space it needs to grow.

aPRIL

GROW IT: Plants

Growing a themed garden can be a lot of fun, and it's a good way to learn plant names. Here are five plants to grow an animal garden. They all have animal-themed names, so add a touch of the wild to your backyard. April is a great time to find plants and get ready to add them to your yard.

Butterfly Weed

Difficulty:

The Basics: Perennial, Zones 4 to 10, up to 3 feet

Grow It: Don't let the name fool you. Butterflies *do* love this plant, but it's not really a weed. Grow from seed by planting directly into the soil after the danger of frost has passed. They like full to partial sun, and you don't need to water them much. In fact, they like conditions that are a little drier.

Top Secret Tip: Be patient. If you plant butterfly weed this year, it might not bloom until next year. But once you get it established it keeps coming back stronger and more beautiful than ever.

Fun Fact: They are toxic, so don't go chewing on them because they could make you sick!

Catmint

Difficulty: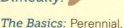

The Basics: Perennial, Zones 5 to 9, up to 12 inches

Grow It: Catmint has beautiful purple flowers all summer! Just sprinkle seeds into the ground in spring and you'll probably get a few purple shoots before the end of the season. Then they'll come back the next year as well. Catmint likes full sun to partial shade and even does well in dry conditions.

Top Secret Tip: If your catmint gets too bushy or full, just cut it back a bit. This will help encourage a second round of growth.

Fun Fact: Cats love this plant. No, it's not catnip, exactly. But if there are outdoor cats around your yard, they might stop by to snack on this plant or just roll around in it. If you have an indoor cat, snip off a few strands to bring inside as a treat.

Tiger Lily

Difficulty:

The Basics: Perennial, Zones 3 to 9, up to 5 feet

Grow It: There are hundreds of different lilies that you can grow, including oriental lilies and hardy lilies. For tiger lilies, which are orange and have black spots, look for the specific botanical name *Lilium lancifolium*. Plant your tiger lily bulbs in full sun.

Top Secret Tip: Some people call tiger lilies ditch lilies because you often seem them growing along the side of the road in ditches. This is because they love wet conditions and water often collects in ditches.

Fun Fact: An old superstition says that if you smell tiger lilies, you will get freckles. Watch out!

Elephant Ear

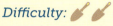

Difficulty: 🌱🌱

The Basics: Perennial, Zones 7 to 11, up to 4 feet

Grow It: It's called elephant ear because the leaves it grows are almost the size of a real elephant's ear! And they are kind of shaped the same, too. This plant grows from a giant tuberous bulb, bigger than a grapefruit. In spring, plant in a spot that gets some sun and some shade. The bulb should be several inches deep.

Top Secret Tip: Most bulbs can't survive over the winter. If you live in a colder region, you need to dig up the bulb in fall and store it in a dry, cool place. Then plant again in spring.

Fun Fact: While you won't see many in home gardens, one kind of elephant ear plant (Borneo Giant) grow up to 15 feet tall! This makes it one of the largest leaf plants in the world.

Hens and Chicks

Difficulty: 🌱🌱

The Basics: Perennial, Zones 4 to 11, just a few inches tall

Grow It: Hens and chicks are related to cactus, so they like dry and sunny conditions. They should get 4 to 6 hours of sunlight per day. Buy plants at your local garden center or look online for cool varieties.

Top Secret Tip: Hens and chicks are a great rock garden plant, and they also do well in containers. So if you have a rocky area or want to try planting them between rocks, this is a good one to try.

Fun Fact: The plant got its name because it looks like it has one large hen, surrounded by smaller little chicks. These hens might not produce eggs, but they are good ones to give away to friends.

More Animal Plants

- Leopard's bane
- Lambs' ear
- Dogwood
- Bee balm
- Spider flower
- Cardinal flower
- Tickseed
- Monkey grass
- Snake's head fritillary
- Butterfly bush
- Dragon's bloom sedum
- Foxglove

PLANT IT: Flowers and Veggies Plan

This season, mix your flowers and veggies together in the same space. Now you can enjoy your pretty blooms and have delicious veggies, too. You only need about a 4' × 4' space for this combination.

Difficulty:

Plants: Cucumbers, zinnias, dwarf sunflowers

The Basics: In this flower/veggie combo, you get to grow up and down. Plant your cucumbers first (a few seeds in 2 to 3 total mounds). Then sprinkle your sunflower and zinnia seeds around it. Thin the flower seeds once they sprout and then keep the area watered so everything grows big and strong.

Cucumbers: Cucumbers are sprawling vegetables, but they are also very versatile. You can move the vines around to adjust to the space you need. They'll grow great underneath the other flowers.

Zinnias: Plant directly in the ground around your cucumber plants. Most will grow 1 to 2 feet tall, leaving plenty of room underneath for the cucumbers.

Dwarf sunflowers: Mammoth sunflowers can get up to 10 feet tall, but dwarf varieties grow 3 to 4 feet. They'll be perfect, just a little bit taller than the zinnias.

Five More Sprawling Veggies

1. Cantaloupe
2. Watermelon
3. Pumpkin
4. Squash
5. Eggplant

Cucumber

Zinnia

Dwarf sunflower

EaT IT:
Creative with Carrots

Carrots are easy to grow, good for you, and delicious! You can also start carrots in spring, summer, and early fall to have several different crops.

Stacy's Secret Family Carrot Cake

Difficulty: 🥄🥄🥄

Yield: 20 servings

4 eggs, separated into whites and yolks

2 cups sugar

1½ cup oil

2 cups flour

2½ teaspoons cinnamon

2 teaspoons baking soda

1 teaspoon salt

3 cups shredded carrots

1 Preheat oven to 350°F.

2 Beat egg whites until they are nice and fluffy, and set aside.

3 In your mixer, cream sugar and oil together. Then add egg yolks, one at a time to the sugar mixture, beating well after each one.

4 In a separate bowl, mix dry ingredients—flour, cinnamon, baking soda, and salt—together.

5 Slowly add dry ingredients to the sugar and oil mixture as you mix on a slow setting.

6 Finally, fold in the egg whites and carrots.

7 Pour mixture into a large 9" × 13" baking pan, greased.

8 Bake for 30 minutes. Let cool in pan for at least 20 minutes before serving.

Carrot Cake Icing

Difficulty:

Yield: 20 servings

8-ounce package cream cheese

2 teaspoons vanilla

3 cups powdered sugar

1 Mix cream cheese, vanilla, and powdered sugar together in a mixer.

2 Ice cake once it's cooled.

Carrot Pizza

Difficulty:

Yield: 8 servings

2 packages refrigerated crescent roll dough

1 cup sour cream

8 ounces cream cheese

1 package ranch mix

2 cups shredded carrots

1 cup shredded cheese

1 Roll out crescent rolls onto cookie sheet and bake according to package.

2 Mix together sour cream, cream cheese, and ranch mix.

3 Once crescent rolls are cooled, spread mixture on top.

4 Then sprinkle carrots and shredded cheese on top.

5 Cut into small squares and enjoy.

Glazed Carrots

Difficulty:

Yield: 2 servings

¼ cup olive oil

¼ cup brown sugar

2 tablespoons ranch salad dressing

2 cups sliced carrots

1 In a medium saucepan, combine olive oil, brown sugar, and ranch dressing.

2 Cook on low heat until everything is mixed together.

3 Next, add carrots and cook on medium heat for about 5 minutes or until carrots are softened and glazed.

Oatmeal Carrot Muffins

Difficulty:

Yield: 24 servings

¾ cup flour

¾ cup oatmeal

½ cup toasted oat bran

1½ teaspoons baking powder

½ teaspoon soda

1 teaspoon cinnamon

¼ teaspoon nutmeg

1 beaten egg

1 cup milk

½ cup brown sugar

¼ cup oil

½ cup shredded carrots

½ cup raisins

½ cup nuts (optional)

1 Preheat oven to 350°F.

2 Mix all ingredients together.

3 Fill muffin tins ⅔ full.

4 Bake for 20 minutes.

Growing Carrots

1. Once the risk of frost has past, plant carrot seeds into soil about ⅜ of an inch deep.
2. Once the carrot seedlings sprout up, thin them out. You'll want to have plants about every inch.
3. Watch your carrot leaves grow taller. After about 8 to 10 weeks, pull the carrots out of the ground, wash them off and then eat them!

Psst! You can eat fresh carrots all summer! Starting in spring, plant new carrot seeds every 2 to 3 weeks for a fresh harvest that will extend all the way into fall!

♻ RECYCLE IT:
Add Life to Your Garden

Old golf balls can be converted into great garden caterpillars you can tuck away in your garden between the plants.

Golf Ball Bugs

Difficulty:

Materials

- ☐ Golf balls
- ☐ Acrylic paint
- ☐ Paintbrushes
- ☐ Fast drying, powerful glue like Super Glue
- ☐ Cork mat
- ☐ Small double-sided adhesive circles, like Glue Dots
- ☐ Craft eyes
- ☐ Paper clips
- ☐ Sharpie marker

1 Clean and dry golf balls

2 Paint your golf balls with acrylic paint—especially a variety meant to be weatherproof. You can use one color or many, if you like. Let dry for at least 1 hour.

3 Carefully glue golf balls to the cork mat and to each other. Position the balls in a zigzag so it looks more like a caterpillar inching along.

4 Using double-sided adhesive, attach craft eyes onto the front of your caterpillar.

5 Unroll a paper clip then wrap it around a pencil to create a coil, and slide it off. Attach this new antenna to your caterpillar one of two ways—using double-sided adhesive or by poking the end of the paper clip into the cork, just behind the caterpillar's head. Repeat with another paper clip for the second antenna.

6 Finally, add other decorations with a marker.

 RECYCLE IT:
Creative Containers

Have you checked out the container section at your local garden center? There are lots of great options, but they can be expensive! You don't need to buy a brand-new container for $20 or $30, though. Instead, just head to your basement, garage, or local thrift store to try one of these projects!.

Unique Container Ideas

- Boots
- Shoes
- Coffee pot
- Teapot
- Milk jug (cut the top off)
- Old soccer ball or basketball
- Pans
- Baskets

DIY Planters

Difficulty:

1 No matter what kind of recycled container you use, you will need to make sure it has good drainage. Depending on what your container is made out of, take a drill and screw or hammer and nail to drill or poke several holes into the bottom of your container. Test it by adding a little water. Keep adding holes until water flows out of the bottom easily, without pooling.

2 If you're working with a big container, pick a home for it first—you don't want to fill it with soil only for it to become too heavy to move!

3 You could use soil directly from your garden, but it's probably a better idea to spend a little extra money and buy a special container soil mix from the garden center. (Container soil is specially formulated with fertilizer good for container plants.)

4 When you're choosing plants for your container, make sure you are combining plants with similar light needs. For instance, you don't want to mix impatiens (a shade-loving flower) with marigolds (they love lots of sun). Do a little research and planning before you plant your containers. You'll have better results overall.

5 When you have soil and plants, begin to fill your container. Make sure you don't have too much soil in the containers when you add your plants. If it looks like your plant's root-ball is going to spill soil over the edge, it's best to add your plant first then fill in afterward.

6 Last but not least, don't forget to water your containers. Containers dry out very quickly. Plan on watering your containers every day, or at the least, every other day. When you do water your plants, do so either in the morning or late in the day. You don't want to water in the hottest part of the day because the water will evaporate and get soaked up too quickly.

MAKE IT: DIY Garden Path

Stepping stones are a must-have in any garden. They give you a place to step without ruining your plants, and they are pretty, too. With these chalkboard stepping stones, you can personalize your garden or create your own message.

Chalkboard Stepping Stones

Difficulty: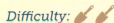

Materials
- [ ] Terra cotta plant saucers (10- to 12-inch)
- [ ] Outdoor paint
- [ ] Paintbrushes
- [ ] Chalkboard paint
- [ ] Chalk

1. Pick up a few plant saucers at your local garden center. Most times, you can buy these separate from the actual terra cotta pot. Clean them up and get them ready for painting.

2. Paint each saucer's backside with an outdoor-friendly paint. You'll want to give it 2 to 3 layers so it will hold up longer.

3. Paint the backside of the saucers with chalkboard paint. You can either paint the entire area or just the inner circle where you'll be stepping (see picture). Again, add a few layers so that it holds up well, and let dry for 2 to 3 hours.

4. Once the paint is all dry, you're ready to add them to your garden. To strengthen the stepping stones, turn them right side up and pack with soil. Then place each one in the spot where you want them.

5. Use chalk to write on the top of the stepping stones. You can change it up anytime you want. Or if it gets smudged, just wipe it off and write something new.

Chalkboard Paint in the Garden

1. **Paint a section of chalkboard on one outside wall of your shed.** You'll want to make sure there's a bit of an overhang to protect it a bit from weather. But if you paint a square, you'll have an instant outdoor activity near the garden.

2. **Make chalkboard flowerpots.** This is also a great way to personalize your plants. Terra cotta is a good surface to paint with chalkboard paint.

3. **Recycle a wooden sign.** You can paint it with chalkboard paint and write a fun garden saying like "Get Growing!"

May

GROW IT: Plants

Don't overlook annuals! They might not last more than one season, but they sure do make your garden beautiful. These are some of the best annuals for backyard gardens. They all look great well into fall, are great for containers and are easy to grow.

Fuchsia

Difficulty:

The Basics: Annual, up to 2 feet tall and 2 feet wide

Grow It: They are very delicate flowers and look great in a hanging basket. Buy a fuchsia plant in spring and place it in a shady area. It really doesn't like to get too hot or have too much sun, so it works better in some sort of container. Then you can move it around.

Top Secret Tip: If temperatures get over 80°F in your area, be sure to place fuchsias in a cooler area.

Fun Fact: Some people call them dancing ladies because they look like a woman with a dress.

Petunia

Difficulty:

The Basics: Annual, up to a foot tall and several feet wide

Grow It: You must have petunias in your garden. They are one of the longest blooming, easiest plants to grow. They look great in flower beds, in containers and more. You can find nearly any color of petunia imaginable. Plant in full sun and be sure to pick the flowers once they're done blooming to encourage even more.

Top Secret Tip: Look for the famous "wave" petunias that gardeners use in containers because they spread well and hang down.

Fun Fact: Dixon, Illinois, is the petunia capital of the world, and every year the city holds a big celebration in this flower's honor.

Coleus

Difficulty:

The Basics: Annual, up to a foot tall and a foot wide

Grow It: The coleus is one of those plants that have hundreds of different varieties. You can find colorful coleuses, plain coleuses, ruffled-leaf coleuses, and giant coleuses. Find coleuses in the shade section of your garden center. This plant does best in lots of shade, and it's a good way to brighten up those areas.

Top Secret Tip: If the leaves get too big, pinch them back. This will keep the plant from getting scraggly.

Fun Fact: You can take a single coleus plant and get twenty or more just by starting new cuttings.

Marigolds

Difficulty: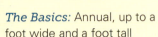

The Basics: Annual, up to a foot wide and a foot tall

Grow It: Marigolds are nearly the opposite of coleuses. While coleus enjoys shade and has no blooms, marigolds love sun and have oodles of flowers. The most common marigold flower color is yellow, but now you can also find orange, red, and others. Sow seeds directly into soil or pick some plants up for cheap at your garden center.

Top Secret Tip: While there's no scientific proof, many gardeners swear that growing marigolds near their veggie plants keeps away bugs and gives them a better, bigger crop.

Fun Fact: For years, people have thought marigold was a cure for things like headaches, toothaches, bee stings, red eyes, and more.

Impatiens

Difficulty:

The Basics: Annual, up to 15 inches wide and tall

Grow It: It's hard to find flowers that actually grow in shade, but impatiens are probably one of the easiest to grow and most popular. Plant them in every shady spot you have, and they'll do great. They are also a popular choice for containers, especially those that sit under eaves or on stoops where sun is almost nonexistent.

Top Secret Tip: Though traditional impatiens are shade plants, the past few years, a new variety has come out that likes sun. So be sure to check which kind you're buying.

Fun Fact: They have the nickname of "touch-me-nots" because the flower seed pods will actually explode when you touch them.

More Popular Annuals

- Geranium
- Begonia
- Pansy
- Salvia
- Zinnia
- Sunflower
- Cosmos
- Hollyhock
- Vinca

PLANT IT:
Prized Petunias Plan

Petunias are one of the best container plants around. They will look great in this trio. Plant in full sun to partial shade for best results. As long as you keep them watered, they will look great all summer.

Difficulty: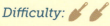

Plants: Wave petunias, sweet potato vine, red star spike

The Basics: You don't need many plants for this combination. With only one spike plant, one sweet potato vine and a four-pack of petunias, you'll have a gorgeous container for months. They all work great in full sun to partial shade, and this container will last into fall, too.

Petunias: Wave petunias are just like they sound; the flowers have a little bit of a wave to them. They also look great in containers and will bloom for months. You can find them in just about any color imaginable, including patterned blooms, stripes and more.

Sweet potato vine: This beautiful trailing plant is perfect for a hanging basket because it will extend your container for several feet. You only need one or two of these to make a big impact.

Red star spike: If you like growing up, then red star spike is a great option. It adds height to your container. Between the red star spike reaching high and sweet potato vine extending below, you could have a container 6 feet tall.

More Spiky Plants

- Yucca
- Agave
- Prickly pear cacti
- Purple majesty millet
- Fountain grass

Wave petunia

Sweet potato vine

Red star spike

EaT IT: Great Green Beans

You can grow many different kinds of green beans in your backyard veggie patch. Just a few green bean plants will give you enough beans to make all of these delicious dishes.

Fresh Veggie Casserole

Difficulty:

Yield: 10 servings

8 small new potatoes

1 cup fresh green beans, snapped

8 baby carrots

3 tablespoons butter

3 tablespoons flour

2 cups milk

Salt and pepper to taste

¾ cup shredded Cheddar cheese

Fresh cilantro

1 Preheat oven to 350°F.

2 Steam potatoes and other vegetables until slightly tender.

3 Arrange veggies in a 2-quart casserole dish. Set aside.

4 Melt butter in a medium sauce pan. Stir in flour until smooth. Then, gradually stir in milk.

5 Cook until thickened, and season to taste with salt and pepper.

6 Add cheese, stirring until cheese is melted.

7 Pour over veggies and sprinkle with cilantro. Bake for 15 minutes.

Green Bean Grill Bites

Difficulty:

Yield: 4 servings

4 cups green beans, snapped and clean

Olive oil or melted butter

Seasonings, to taste, including bacon bits, garlic salt, ranch seasoning, oregano, salt, and pepper.

1 Preheat grill to a low or medium heat.

2 Divide 4 cups green beans into individual 1-cup servings. Place each serving of green beans inside its own large sheet of aluminum foil.

3 Drizzle with olive oil or melted butter and then season to taste.

4 Grill for about 7 minutes on each side or until green beans are tender.

Stir-Fry Green Beans

Difficulty:

Yield: 4 servings

3 cups green beans, cleaned and snapped

¼ cup water

Soy sauce, to taste

Salt and pepper, to taste

Garlic, to taste

1 Add beans, water, soy sauce, salt, pepper, and garlic to skillet.

2 Put lid on skillet and let steam over medium heat for 10 minutes.

Tips for Growing Green Beans

- Green beans like warm, sunny locations.
- Start your green beans inside in peat pots or small cups. They are relatively easy to start indoors. Or you can wait until the danger of frost has passed and plant outside.
- It's important to keep beans watered. This will keep them growing strong.
- When picking beans, don't pull hard. Be gentle so the plants will continue to produce.
- To test a bean to see if it's ready, try snapping one in half. This is where the term "snapping beans" comes from. Beans with a snap to them will taste best.

♻ RECYCLE IT: Serve It Up

Reuse an old tennis racket from a friend or find one for $1 or $2 at your local thrift store. Soon, you'll have a new piece of garden art that will be a beautiful accent for many seasons to come.

Tennis Racket Garden Art

Difficulty: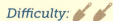

Materials

- Scissors
- Tennis or badminton racket
- Tweezers or needle-nose pliers (optional)
- Ribbon, yarn, wire, or string
- Beads and/or trinkets

1 Using scissors, cut the strings out of the racket. Remove all the strings. (You might want to use some tweezers or needle-nose pliers to get at those hard-to-reach spots.)

2 Measure and cut your ribbon or string to the desired lengths. These will hang down from the top of your racket, so measure twice and cut once.

3 Tie knots at one end of your ribbon. Then string with decorations like colorful beads or wood trinkets.

4 Once you've strung the ribbons, pull them through the holes of the tennis racket and secure with knots. You can leave the beads hanging freely or tie them from one side to another to create a web.

5 Push the racket handle into the ground, and enjoy!

Be a Designer

Be creative with your design. See if you can figure out how to spell out a message across the racket or make a design like a cat! Or raid your cupboards for a little inspiration. For example, noodles are great for stringing and cheap, too! (Noodles might only hold up for a single season, but then that will give you a reason to do another design.) Here's another idea: give your racket a new look with colorful outdoor paint.

♻ RECYCLE IT:
Order in the Garden

It doesn't take long for your garden tools, seeds and other backyard items to turn into clutter in your drawers, garage, and shed. Here are a few ideas to help you stay organized.

Tackle-the-Garden Box

Difficulty: 🛠

Materials
- [ ] Old tackle box
- [ ] Letters, stickers, and other decorative items
- [ ] Garden gloves, tools, and other supplies

1. Clean up an old tackle box.

2. Decorate the outside of the box with letters and stickers.

3. Fill up your tackle box with garden gloves, tools, string, and other small items that you use.

4. Keep your garden box close at hand. This is an easy way to keep the tools you need and use every day close at hand. And you can paint it or decorate it any way you want!

Over-the-Door Cubbies

Difficulty:

Materials

- Over-the-door shoe organizer
- Material swatches for labeling cubbies
- Seed packets, gardening tools, etc.

1 Over-the-door shoe organizers aren't just for shoes. Place one over the door in your garden shed or nail it up on a wall in your garage.

2 Label the cubbies of the organizer with markers or colorful swatches of material so you can see what you have at a glance and keep track of what goes where.

3 Store seed packets, tools, garden shoes and more in your organizer. You have lots of spots to fill, so get to work!

A Gardener's Bulletin Board

Difficulty:

Materials

- Bulletin board
- Lettering from a craft store
- Paper, seed packets

1 Bulletin boards deserve a spot outside, too. Find a spot to hang one on a garden shed, indoors or even on your house (make sure it's under an eave, though).

2 Use lettering from a craft store or make your own to name.

3 Tack up the seed packets you planted with notes of where you put them.

4 Remember to add notes throughout the season on what's growing well, what needs more water, etc. Then keep the bulletin board until next year and you can get a start on the season.

Shoebox Solutions

Difficulty:

Materials
- ☐ Shoebox
- ☐ Seeds and garden supplies

1 Label shoeboxes with whatever garden supplies you are going to put inside. Shoes, seed packets, fertilizer and tools are all good items to include.

2 Stack the shoeboxes in a convenient location. You won't need to keep most garden items—like seeds and seed starting supplies—for long, so this is a great way to store them away.

Spice Jar Seed Storage

Difficulty:

Materials
- ☐ Recycled spice jars
- ☐ Markers

1 Once you finish using a spice jar in the kitchen, save it and clean it out.

2 When you're harvesting seeds from your plants, use the spice jars to collect and store the seeds once they're dry.

3 Label the outside of the jars carefully with markers. Many seeds are good for years to come, so you can save a lot of money by harvesting and storing your own.

Make It: Personalized Containers for Your Plants

Parents and grandparents love personalized gifts! These thumbprint flower-pots are fun to make and are keepsakes your family will appreciate for years to come.

Creative with Fingerprints

Fingerprint animals and art is a lot more popular than you might think. Do an online search for "fingerprint animals" and you'll get some easy ideas as to what you can make with just a few squiggles.

Thumbprint Flowerpots

Difficulty: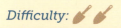

Materials

- [ ] Flowerpots
- [ ] Outdoor paint
- [ ] Markers
- [ ] Newspaper

1 Buy pots at your local garden center. Make sure the pots have a nice smooth surface for making prints. A bumpy or textured surface might be pretty but won't be the best for little fingers.

2 If you do want to paint your flowerpot, this is the time to do it. Apply an outdoor-friendly paint and give it plenty of time to dry.

3 Once your flowerpots are dry, choose a contrasting paint for the prints. Place your thumb into the paint and gently press it onto the pot. (You might want to do a few practice runs first on a piece of newspaper so you get a feel for the paint and how hard to press.)

4 If you do mess up, just wipe off paint immediately and try again.

5 Once the prints are dry, it's time to decorate them. Use markers to turn your prints into animals. Add tails, legs and other little details to make them come alive. Let your imagination be your limit, and again, do some test runs first to make sure it's going to turn out.

6 You can also use fingerprints, handprints, and footprints to make personalized animal shapes.

7 If you're giving this as a gift, go ahead and plant something in your pot when it's dry. It will be perfect for the garden lover in your life!

Ideas for Fingerprint Shapes

- Flowers
- Spiders
- Caterpillars
- Monkey
- Butterfly
- Fish
- Bird

JUNe

GROW IT: Plants

Do you have shade in your backyard? If you do, then you know how hard it can be to get plants to grow there. For those shady areas where the sun doesn't shine much, try some of these plants.

Balloon Flower

Difficulty:

The Basics: Perennial, Zones 4 to 9, up to 1 foot tall

Grow It: This plant might be little, but it has lots of blooms from midsummer to early fall. Find plants at your local garden center or plant seeds in mid-spring. They like a mix of sun and shade.

Top Secret Tip: Be careful in spring when you're weeding. Balloon flowers don't bloom until mid-summer, so it would be easy to think it's just a weed.

Fun Fact: This flower gets its name because it looks like a balloon just before the petals unfold.

Daylily

Difficulty:

The Basics: Perennial, Zones 3 to 9, up to 2 feet tall

Grow It: Daylilies only bloom for a single day, but they're still worth growing! They have beautiful flowers, and they often smell really good, too. Plant daylilies in shade (they'll also do fine in sun). You can find daylilies in almost any color, so look around to find some that you really like.

Top Secret Tip: Save yourself some money and transplant daylilies from a friend. They transplant well and will spread over the years. You should divide them every 3 to 4 years.

Fun Fact: Many daylilies have unique names like Pardon Me and King George. Check out the name whenever you buy one.

Hosta

Difficulty:

The Basics: Perennial, Zones 3 to 8, up to 2 feet tall

Grow It: Every shady spot deserves some hostas. These are great plants to group together. They'll do fine in heavy shade, and nowadays, there are hundreds of different hosta options to choose from. Plant in spring.

Top Secret Tip: Most people don't think of hostas for their blooms, but they do have small flowers that shoot up in summer. They are small, but they still provide great nectar for hummingbirds and butterflies.

Fun Fact: You can find dozens and dozens of special hosta societies. This is one popular plant!

Columbine

Difficulty:

The Basics: Perennial, Zones 3 to 9, up to 2 feet tall

Grow It: This beautiful flower does best in partial shade. Sow seeds directly in spring. They will produce flowers the following year, but they are worth the wait. The flowers are beautiful and unique.

Top Secret Tip: If you plant them in a spot with more sun, make sure they get plenty of water.

Fun Fact: A specific columbine variety, Rocky Mountain columbine, is a mix of purplish blue and white. It is the official state flower of Colorado.

Coral Bells

Difficulty:

The Basics: Perennial, Zones 3 to 9, up to 3 feet tall

Grow It: Coral bells are great foliage plants, and you can find them with green, brown, orange, purple, and pink leaves. They also have small flowers that hang on tall shoots from the leaves. Plant in spring. They prefer some shade but do really well in semi-shaded areas, too.

Top Secret Tip: The small flowers of coral bells make a great cutting. Snip them off and put them in a vase in summer.

Fun Fact: This is another one with fun variety names. Look for things like Amber Waves, Midnight Rose, and Black Beauty.

More Great Shade Picks

- Phlox
- Ferns
- Caladium
- Coleus
- Lily of the valley
- Astilbe
- Bleeding heart
- Lungwort

PLANT IT:
Salsa Garden Plan

Follow this garden plan and then you'll be able to make fresh garden salsa later in the summer. You can grow these all in containers if you don't have the space (though it would only take roughly a 3' × 3' space). For a creative gift idea, package up seeds or plants. Then include instructions for growing these plants and the recipe for salsa. The gardener in your life will love this.

Difficulty:

Plants: Tomatoes, peppers, onions, cilantro

The Basics: Plant a couple of tomato plants, two or three pepper plants, four to six onions, and just a couple of cilantro plants. This is all you need to make a dozen or more jars of salsa. Grow in full sun. Or if growing in containers, tomatoes and peppers should have their own containers, while onions and cilantro can be paired up with several together.

Tomatoes: A couple of tomato plants go a long way. You shouldn't need more than two or three tomato plants to have enough to make salsa. Roma tomatoes or large varieties are best for salsa.

Peppers: You choose the kind of peppers you want for salsa. Bell peppers are a must, but you might also want to add banana peppers or jalapeños if you like your salsa a little hot.

Onions: Onions are optional, but they are also great in fresh salsa. If you plant your onions earlier in the season, store them in a cool spot until the tomatoes and peppers are ready to harvest.

Cilantro: Grow cilantro along the edge of your garden. You can use it to flavor lots of summer veggies, and it's a must-have addition in salsa.

Making Salsa

Follow the Fresh Tomato and Pepper Salsa recipe later in this chapter. If you don't have all of these ingredients in your garden at the same time, visit your local farmers' market.

Tomato

Pepper

Onion

Cilantro

EAT IT: Perfect Peppers

Whether you like hot peppers, sweet peppers, or some in between, they are great in lots of recipes. Add a few to your favorite dish or try them with some of these.

Chicken Pepper Enchilada Dip

Difficulty:

Yield: 16 servings

1 pound chicken breast, chopped

1 (8-ounce) package cream cheese

1 (8-ounce) jar mayonnaise

1 (8-ounce) package shredded Cheddar cheese

¼ cup green bell peppers, chopped

¼ cup red bell peppers, chopped

2 tablespoons jalapeño peppers

1   Combine ingredients in slow cooker and heat on low for 2 to 3 hours.

2   Serve with tortilla chips.

Fresh Tomato and Pepper Salsa

Difficulty:

Yield: 10 servings

4 cups chopped tomatoes

½ cup chopped bell peppers

¼ cup chopped jalapeños

½ cup chopped onions

2 tablespoons fresh chopped cilantro

1 teaspoon salt

2 teaspoons minced garlic

Juice of 1 lime

1 Mix all ingredients together and refrigerate for at least an hour to get better flavor.

2 The longer the salsa sits, the more flavorful it will be. It will stay good for 2 to 3 days.

Taco Stuffed Peppers

Difficulty:

Yield: 4 servings

4 bell peppers

1 pound ground turkey

1 taco seasoning package

1 cup shredded cheese

Fresh Tomato and Pepper Salsa

Sour cream

1 Cut the tops off your green peppers and clean out the seeds.

2 Boil water in a large pot. Drop peppers in to boil them. The peppers should be in the boiling water for 4 to 6 minutes. Carefully remove the peppers from water and set aside.

3 Meanwhile, brown ground turkey in a medium pan.

4 Add taco seasoning pack and follow directions on the back for how much water to add, and simmer for 5 to 10 minutes.

5 Remove ground turkey from heat and fill green peppers.

6 Top with shredded cheese, salsa, and sour cream.

Cheesy Pepper Pizza

Difficulty:

Yield: 6 servings

Pizza dough, your own, a mix, or premade

1 cup pizza sauce

2 cups mozzarella cheese

1 cup fresh-cut bell peppers

1 Preheat the oven to 400°F.

2 Press dough out on to a pizza pan.

3 Add pizza sauce on top and top with mozzarella cheese and peppers.

4 Bake for 10 to 15 minutes.

Playing with Your Food!

Peppers are a fun veggie. When you cut them, you can make all kinds of shapes. Cut them into rings to make bracelets or pull the sides of the ring together for a butterfly shape. Another idea is to cut them vertically to make "J" shapes. See what other shapes you can make with peppers.

Going on a Bug Hunt

Whether you're going on a daytime or nighttime bug hunt, summer is the prime time to explore the little crawlers in your yard.

Bug Checklist

See if you can spot these common bugs in your yard.

- Ladybug
- Spider
- Butterfly
- Caterpillar
- Ant
- Beetle

Bug Hunting Gear

Difficulty:

Materials

- Clear jar or plastic container
- Magnifying glass
- Long spoon
- Gloves
- Notepad

1   First off, you need something for your bugs to call home (temporarily of course). Decorate a clear jar or plastic container and add air holes to the top. Bugs need to breathe!

2   If you go bug hunting during the day, don't forget a magnifying glass. This is a good way to spot even the tiniest bugs. Don't forget to search everywhere— under leaves, under rocks, on trees and more.

3   When you do find a bug, give it a good look. Though most are harmless, you might want to wear gloves and use a spoon to scoop it up. Every once in a while, you might find one that stings or bites.

4   If you're going to keep a bug and observe it for a little while, gently put it in your container or jar and close the lid. Don't keep it for more than 10 or 15 minutes or so. Just have it in there long enough to observe its behaviors. Remember that you wouldn't like someone keeping you contained in a jar! When you're done looking at it, make sure you put it back where you found it.

5   Try to identify bugs that you find. Use your notepad to take notes about it and write down what you see. Was it a spider or an insect? How many legs did it have? Could it fly? These are all things to keep an eye out for when exploring bugs.

6   Finally, don't forget to search for bugs at night, too. Lightning bugs are the obvious choice. They start coming out just before it gets dark. But also keep an eye out for moths. They are attracted to light and are very interesting to see up close.

Try your hand at composting by letting worms do all of the work! This is a great introduction to how composting works, and you get to get your hands dirty, too.

Worm Compost Bin

Difficulty: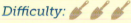

Materials

- [ ] Bin with lid (bucket, plastic container, etc.)
- [ ] Drill and bit
- [ ] Bedding material (mix of soil with newspaper or leaves)
- [ ] Redworms, ask for them at your local tackle shop. Do not use earthworms from your backyard. These are not the kind of worms that can compost.

1 Drill small holes in the sides of the bin with a ¹⁄₁₆-inch drill bit. This step is very important because the worms need air to survive.

2 Create a bed in the bottom of the bin. Slightly dampen your newspaper or leaves, then mix with a good garden soil. Fill the bin about ¾ of the way full. Then add your worms on top.

3 Give the worms a few days to settle into their new home. Once they do, start adding veggie scraps under the surface of the bedding. Be careful not to feed them too much. A good rule of thumb is 20 parts "brown" material to 1 part "green" material. You might get compost in as little as a few weeks. Then when you want to start a new bed of compost, move the worms from one bin to another.

Green vs. Brown

So what is green material versus brown? Green materials are generally softer, like kitchen scraps, coffee grounds, and grass clippings. Brown materials are coarser, like paper products and leaves.

Worm Composting vs. Regular Composting

Worm composting lets the worms do all the work of mixing up your materials. They eat the garbage and then poop out great compost with lots of nutrients! On the other hand, a traditional compost bin needs to be turned or mixed up by you. It slowly breaks down, and the results are compost.

DO Compost . . .

- Grass clippings
- Leaves
- Weeds and garden debris
- Small brush
- Twigs
- Wood ash
- Sawdust
- Wood chips
- Egg shells
- Coffee grounds

DO NOT Compost . . .

- Meat
- Bones
- Fat
- Dairy products
- Oils
- Whole branches, logs
- Pet or human waste
- Ash from treated wood

Make It:
The Natural Artist

Art and nature go hand in hand. And when you paint outside, it makes for easy cleanup because the water hose is nearby. One thing is for sure—after you do this project, you'll see the details of your backyard in a whole new way.

More Nature Objects for Painting

- Rocks
- Twigs
- Bark
- Acorn
- Helicopter seeds

Plant Stamps and Brushes

Difficulty:

1 Look around your backyard for plants that might be good for painting. Long grasses make great paintbrushes, large leaves are good for stamping shapes, and flower petals can be good for detail work.

2 On a paper plate, squirt out a few colors of paint. Then put out a piece of paper you'll use as your canvas.

3 Dip grasses into the paint and add a few strokes across your paper. Compare the paint stroke of a wispy grass to that of a stiff one, and see which one creates the look you want.

4 Also test other plants as stamps and finer brushes. Try short and tall plants, ones with new shapes, and more. It might take a few times to get it just right.

5 Once you've finished your picture, hang it up in the sun to dry. Cleanup is easy—just get out the water hose and spray it away (make sure you were using a water-based paint).

JULY

GROW IT: Plants

Are you looking for the easiest, most beautiful perennials for your backyard? Here they are! All of these are only rated one spade because they are simple to grow and look great.

Shasta Daisy

Difficulty:

The Basics: Perennial, Zones 5 to 9, up to 3 feet tall

Grow It: These are classic daisies that grow well in just about every soil type. Plant in a sunny spot in spring; the blooms will start to come out when the weather is warm.

Top Secret Tip: Shasta daisies bloom all summer, and they are great for a cutting. Snip off a few to place in a vase. It's a good way to bring the outside inside. This also encourages a healthy plant because when you snip off a flower, it sends nutrients down into the plant to store. Snip off just a few or several; this plant usually has several to spare.

Fun Fact: This plant was named after Mount Shasta in California where flower developer Luther Burbank created the daisy more than 100 years ago!

Black-Eyed Susan

Difficulty:

The Basics: Perennial, Zones 3 to 9, up to 3 feet tall

Grow It: These plants are easy to grow, they do well in dry conditions and they are one of the longest-blooming plants in the garden. Plant in a sunny spot in early spring.

Top Secret Tip: Butterflies love this plant! The most common flower color is yellow, but you should also look for cool new varieties that come in red, multicolor, and double blooms.

Fun Fact: Take a close look at this plant. The name "black-eyed" actually refers to the flower's dark brown (not black) centers.

Purple Coneflower

Difficulty:

The Basics: Perennial, Zones 3 to 9, up to 3 feet tall

Grow It: Coneflowers are one of the most popular garden plants right now. Butterflies love them, they'll grow great in sun or partial shade, and they are sturdy plants! You rarely see them droop or fall over. Add plants or seeds in spring.

Top Secret Tip: While the classic color is pink, coneflowers come in orange, yellow, red, and even green. Most of these newer varieties don't last every year, but they sure are fun to try!

Fun Fact: Lots of people call this plant by its botanical name, Echinacea. Echinacea is still sold today in health or vitamin stores to help strengthen your immune system.

Bee Balm

Difficulty:

The Basics: Perennial, Zones 4 to 9, up to 3 feet tall

Grow It: These plants have fun spiky flowers that bees, hummingbirds, and butterflies all love! Plant in full sun or partial shade in spring. Make sure you give these plants plenty of space (12 to 15 inches apart) so they don't get the plant disease powdery mildew.

Top Secret Tip: After bee balm finishes blooming, cut it back right away. With the right conditions, this might encourage it to bloom again!

Fun Fact: Oswego tea comes from bee balm flowers and leaves. This is an age-old tea that early immigrants learned how to make from the Oswego Native American tribe.

Garden Phlox

Difficulty:

The Basics: Perennial, Zones 4 to 9, up to 3 feet tall

Grow It: The fastest and easiest way to grow phlox is to find someone who already has some. Divide a clump in early spring and plant in full sun. Or you can also add plants or seeds at this time. Phlox can have more than 100 blooms on a single plant.

Top Secret Tip: Don't confuse garden phlox (mentioned here) to creeping phlox. Both are good choices for the garden, but garden phlox grows tall, while creeping phlox is more of a groundcover.

Fun Fact: The name phlox comes from the Greek word that means flame. So think of this plant as having tiny little flames all over.

Growing Grass

No, not the green grass you grow in your lawn. Ornamental grasses might be one of the most overlooked perennials in the backyard. But they look great with anything and are very reliable. Don't think grasses are boring, either. They have interesting color and cool texture. Here are some top grasses to try.

- Fountain grass
- Blue fescue
- Feather reed grass
- Flame grass
- Pampas grass
- Ribbon grass
- Switch grass
- Zebra grass

PLANT IT:
Patriotic Container Plan

You can have a patriotic display in your garden around the Fourth of July with this container plan. Add a flag, and it will make a great holiday display. You might also try adding ribbons, beads or other red, white, and blue accessories.

Difficulty:

Plants: Pansies, salvia, dusty miller

The Basics: These plants all do great in sun to partial shade. You can mix and match the quantity of these plants to your personal taste, but you probably only need one to three of each one. For the best red, white, and blue display, buy plants fresh from your garden center a couple of weeks before the Fourth.

Pansies: Look for blue-hued pansies to add to your container. If you can't find blue ones, look for other blue bloomers at your garden center. You might be able to find petunias in blue as well.

Salvia: These are bright red annuals that do great in containers. You can buy them all season at your garden center, so add some in May or July; they'll do great.

Dusty miller: They are plants grown for their foliage that have a white-green look to them.

Get the Blues

Blue blooms are the hardest to find. Here are a few other blue options.

- Blue hydrangea
- Bellflowers
- Blue mistflower
- Forget-me-nots
- Bluebells
- Bluebonnets
- Morning glory
- Bearded iris

Pansy

Salvia

Dusty miller

eat IT: Tasty Tomatoes

Tomatoes are all-stars in summer's vegetable garden. There's nothing like a fresh tomato you've grown yourself. Here are a few recipes that will help you work your way through the abundant red veggies!

Holy Moly Guacamole

Difficulty:

Yield: 8 servings

3 avocados, mashed

2 limes, juiced

1 teaspoon salt

3 tablespoons chopped cilantro

1 cup fresh chopped tomatoes

1 teaspoon minced garlic

1 Mix all ingredients together in a medium bowl.

2 Refrigerate 1 hour for best flavor or serve immediately.

Fresh Tomato and Basil Bruschetta

Difficulty:

Yield: 12 servings

2 cups fresh diced tomatoes

¼ cup fresh basil, chopped

1 teaspoon minced garlic

2 teaspoons balsamic vinegar

1 teaspoon olive oil

Salt and pepper to taste

¼ cup grated Parmesan cheese

French bread

1 Combine all ingredients except bread in medium bowl.

2 Stir well and serve over French bread.

Tomato Cups

Difficulty:

Yield: 4 servings

4 fresh tomatoes

1 can tuna

½ cup mayonnaise

¼ cup celery

¼ cup dried, sweetened cranberries

1 Chop the top off your tomatoes and carefully clean out the inside and discard to your compost pile. (This is the hardest part to the whole thing.)

2 You want to hollow them out so you can put the tuna mixture inside, so do the best you can.

3 Mix tuna, mayonnaise, celery, and cranberries together in a bowl.

4 Fill tomatoes with the mixture and eat.

5 Larger tomatoes are good if you're doing this as a meal. Smaller tomatoes work well if this is an appetizer.

Taco Dip

Yield: 8 servings

1 package reduced-fat
cream cheese

1 (8-ounce) carton
reduced-fat sour cream

1 package taco seasoning

3 cups chopped lettuce

1 cup fresh chopped
tomatoes

2 cups finely shredded
cheese

Tortilla chips

1 Mix cream cheese, sour cream, and taco seasoning
in a small bowl.

2 Spread the mixture into a round serving dish, about
the size of a large pizza pan.

3 Sprinkle lettuce, fresh tomatoes and cheese on top.

4 Eat as a dip with tortilla chips. (Guacamole is good on
this, too. Just add a guacamole layer after the sour
cream layer.)

Tips for Growing Tomatoes

- You can find lots of different varieties these days from cherry and plum to beefsteak ones. They even make chocolate miniature tomatoes. Try growing two to three different kinds so you can taste a few.
- Don't forget to water your plants! This will really make a difference in the long run. Just get in the habit of watering at the same time every day so you don't forget.
- You need sun. Don't think you can grow tomatoes in shade. If you don't have lots of sunny spots, try growing tomatoes in a container instead and placing in the sun.
- Get a good support system. When they are mature, tomatoes could have nearly 100 pounds of fruit growing on them. Get a good tomato support for yours.
- Harvest regularly. When you keep harvesting your tomatoes, you will encourage the plants to keep producing.
- Save the green ones. At the end of the season, you can save a few green tomatoes and let them ripen over fall. Give it a try.

 RECYCLE IT:
Decorating in the Garden

It's time to get creative! Turn ordinary indoor and outdoor objects into great garden art. Here are five ideas to try in your backyard using recycled objects. What else can you come up with?

Picture Frame Flower Art

Difficulty:

Materials
- Picture frame
- Paint
- Vase
- String
- Flowers

1 Take the glass and/or plastic out of the picture frame. (In this example pictured here, it's a 16" × 20" frame.

2 Clean up the picture frame and paint it your favorite color with an outdoor paint.

3 Now you're going to secure the frame to the vase from the top using string. You'll have to put holes in the top so you have something to tie to. Suspend the vase from the frame so it appears to be floating in air.

4 Put fresh-cut flowers in your makeshift vase and add water. Hang in a tree or against your shed. Change out the flowers by season.

Golf Club Flag

Difficulty:

Materials
- Golf club
- String
- Outdoor flag

1 Hang an old golf club in a tree using string or twine. Hang it horizontally to display the flag evenly.

2 Secure a garden flag to it to make your yard festive. Change out the flags as you'd like.

Container Skirt

Difficulty:

Materials
- [ ] Old rain coat, shower curtain, or other water-resistant material
- [ ] Measuring tape
- [ ] Glue (optional)

1 Measure your container first; if you're careful, you can probably get several container skirts from a single shower curtain.

2 Tuck the material around the bottom and edges of a plain container. You can secure it with glue, if needed, but you should be able to just tuck as needed.

3 Change out your container skirt as much as you'd like. This is great way to take your patriotic container one step further or to accent a colorful container.

Pictures in the Garden

Difficulty:

Materials
- [ ] Picture frame
- [ ] Wire (2–3 feet)
- [ ] Metal stake
- [ ] Beads

1 Who says you can't put pictures in the garden? Hang frames on your shed or plant a wrought iron frame. To start with take a small frame and put in a picture.

2 Attach the frame to a metal stake using wire. The metal stake will make it easy to push into the ground.

3 Use additional wire to decorate your frame and to string beads. You can use a variety of frames, but wrought iron is a good choice in this because it will hold up in nearly any kind of weather. This makes a great gift for grandparents!

Garden Tool Greats

Difficulty:

Materials

- [ ] Old gardening tools
- [ ] Magnetic alphabet letters

1 Old shovels, garden hoes, and more can be used as garden art once they're rusty or busted.

2 Put a shovel up in your garden. Then use magnetic alphabet letters to write a message or decorate.

3 Look for other magnets to use on old garden tools as well. It's an easy way to add some color and fun in the garden for free.

MAKE IT:
'Tis the Growing Season

By July, you probably have a yard full of beautiful flowers, and it's the peak of the season. Document your beautiful space through photos and turn some of your hard work into cards for your family and friends.

Garden Cards

Difficulty: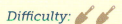

Materials

- ☐ Camera
- ☐ Flowers
- ☐ Quote book
- ☐ Cardstock paper
- ☐ Glue
- ☐ Scissors
- ☐ Yarn, buttons and other art adornments

1. Get to know your camera. Try out the macro feature on it and see if it makes a difference. Take pictures close up and far away to see what gets the best results. Keep practicing until you get ones you want to use.

2. Select your favorite pictures and print them yourself, or have them printed at a local store.

3. Glue your pictures onto the paper and adorn with fun objects. From yarn and buttons to stickers and more—anything goes!

4. Check out a quote book from your local library or go online to look for quotes. Search for words like "growing," "gardens," "spring," and "summer." Many of these will really go along great with your flower photos.

5. Write your message on your card.

6. Deliver your cards personally or send via snail mail (keep in mind that you might need special envelopes and extra postage).

7. Think about what else you could do with the photos from your garden—turn them into a picture video, send a virtual e-card or even make a poster collage.

Make It: Saving Summer's Splendor

Keep your flowers for months and years longer by pressing and preserving them. Then transform them into artwork, cards or bookmarks.

Pressed Flowers

Difficulty:

Materials

- [ ] Flowers
- [ ] Leaves and foliage
- [ ] Heavy book
- [ ] Tissue
- [ ] Newspaper
- [ ] Hand weights

1. Collect flowers midmorning. They will have dew on them earlier, but be too dry later in the day.

2. When you cut flowers, snip off the entire flower and stem. It's better to have too much than too little. You may want to dig out the entire root system for some because those can be pressed as well.

3. Press the flowers as flat as possible. You may have to remove the center of the flower and realign the petals to flatten them completely.

4. Place flattened flowers between two pieces of tissue or tissue paper. Put a layer of newspaper on either side and set inside a sturdy book. Phone books will work; hardcover encyclopedia-type books work even better.

5. To speed the drying process, pop your book in the microwave and zap it for 30 to 45 seconds.

6. Lay the book down and stack weight on top. Other books will work, but hand weights are less bulky.

7. After 2 to 4 weeks your flowers will be pressed. Apply them onto cards, bookmarks or paper.

AUGUST

GROW IT: Plants

These popular annuals look great in the garden, require very little care from you, and are easy to grow (all just one spade), so they definitely deserve a spot in your garden. Plant in spring, and they'll keep growing, growing, growing all the way into fall.

Cosmos

Difficulty:

The Basics: Annual, up to 4 to 5 feet tall

Grow It: Cosmos are easy to grow. Just sprinkle them in the ground and you'll likely get about 80 percent of the seeds that germinate. Thin seedlings out every 6 to 8 inches or so. Don't overwater these plants; they like it dry.

Top Secret Tip: Look for cosmos with interesting features like seashell cosmos's unique flower petals, candy stripe cosmos's pink and white stripes, and chocolate cosmos's smell of—yes, it's true—chocolate!

Fun Fact: Balance your garden—cosmos come from the Greek word that means "balanced universe."

Spider Flower

Difficulty:

The Basics: Annual, up to 4 feet tall

Grow It: Also called cleome, spider flowers bloom in early summer until fall. Sprinkle a few seeds in the ground as soon as the danger of frost has passed. They will do okay in dry conditions, but they prefer lots of sun and a good source of water.

Top Secret Tip: Mix up your cleome. They look great in groups, so sprinkle several different kinds of cleome seed in one spot.

Fun Fact: Even though they are annuals, these plants might actually reseed themselves. This means they will drop their seeds one season and sprout again the next year.

Sunflowers

Difficulty:

The Basics: Annual, 2 to 10+ feet tall

Grow It: Sunflowers are a must! You can grow huge varieties (Russian Mammoth grow 8 to 10 feet tall), a dwarf mix (a few feet tall), or unique blooms like Teddy Bear sunflowers (they're fuzzy). Sow seeds directly into the ground in a location where they'll get lots and lots of sun!

Top Secret Tip: Sunflower heads can get really heavy. Give them some support or cut off the tops before they droop over and break the stem.

Fun Fact: Harvest sunflower seeds for yourself or leave them for the birds. Either way, cut the head off a large sunflower head and let it dry. Once the seeds dry, pop them out to eat or hang it back outside for the birds.

Zinnias

Difficulty:

The Basics: Annual, up to 3 feet tall

Grow It: You can buy zinnia plants at your local garden center or start seeds indoors a few weeks before it's time to plant outside. Make sure you put these in a good location; they like lots of sun!

Top Secret Tip: Butterflies love these plants. They are a great addition to a butterfly garden. Mix these in with other butterfly favorites and you should have lots of monarchs, swallowtails, and more stopping by!

Fun Fact: Zinnias were originally thought of as ugly eyesores because they looked weedy. But plant botanists eventually developed the gorgeous flowers we know and love today.

Morning Glory

Difficulty:

The Basics: Annual, up to 10 feet long

Grow It: This annual is considered a vine because it climbs 6 to 10 feet over walls, trellises, posts, etc. Plant directly into the ground in full sun. Make sure that it has something to grow up. Morning glories have one of the few blue blooms available for backyard gardens. Look for the Heavenly Blue variety.

Top Secret Tip: It's really important to make sure this plant has something to grow up. Otherwise, they could attach themselves to your other plants and choke them out. If you can give them their own space, that would be best.

Fun Fact: They get their name because the blooms often bloom in the morning and then fade away in the afternoon.

Superpower Annuals

While most annuals are just good for a year, here are a few that will often reseed themselves.

- Four o'clocks
- Marigolds
- Cosmos
- Cleome
- Morning glory
- Salvia
- Snapdragon
- Coreopsis

PLANT IT:
Growing Tall Plan

Create a plant hideaway in your backyard with these tall, gorgeous plants. Find a space in your yard, draw a large circle and then plant the seeds along the circle. As the plants grow upward, it'll create a hidden space within. Once the plants are a few feet tall, you can stake the plants, leaving a "doorway" opening. This will give you an interesting garden playhouse and secure the plants.

Difficulty:

Plants: Sunflowers, cosmos, zinnias

The Basics: After your plants begin to grow, the most important thing to remember is to give them space. You want to grow several sunflowers, cosmos, and zinnias, but don't let them crowd each other out. The best way to avoid this is by making a large circle so the plants still have room to spread out a bit. At the least, they should be 6 to 8 inches apart and in full sun.

Sunflowers: Choose a tall variety of sunflowers for this garden plan. The stakes you use will give the stems support, and the leaves will add cover for your hideaway.

Cosmos: These don't really require support, but they do make good companions with sunflowers. Between these two, you should be able to create a distinct, rounded bed.

Zinnias: They aren't nearly as tall as the other two, but they'll create a nice, lower layer of blooms.

More Tall Perennial Flowers

- Globe thistle
- Hollyhock
- Lily
- Lupine
- Canna lily

Sunflower

Cosmo

Zinnia

eat it:
Craving Cucumbers

When you grow cucumbers, the most important thing is not to let them get too big. Before they do, pluck them off the vine so they'll be yummy in recipes like these.

Cucumber Bites

Difficulty:
Yield: 30 servings

2 large cucumbers

2 cups sour cream

Ranch dip mix

Diced tomatoes

Diced parsley

¼ cup Parmesan cheese

1 Peel cucumbers and then slice them diagonally into coin shapes.

2 Mix sour cream and ranch dip together.

3 Lay the cucumbers out flat on a serving plate and put a small dab of sour cream onto the middle of the cucumber.

4 Garnish with tomatoes, parsley, and Parmesan cheese and serve as an appetizer.

Cucumber Salad

Difficulty:
Yield: 4 servings

2 cups cottage cheese

1 cup chopped cucumbers

1 teaspoon salt

1 teaspoon pepper

½ cup chopped bell peppers

½ cup chopped tomatoes

1 Combine all ingredients and stir together.

2 Eat this salad right away or let it chill for a bit.

3 You can also add other garden-fresh ingredients as you see fit.

Cucumber Lasagna

Difficulty:
Yield: 6 servings

3 cups sliced cucumbers

3 large sliced tomatoes

¾ cup Ranch dressing

½ cup mozzarella cheese

1 Layer sliced cucumbers on bottom of bowl.

2 Follow that with a layer of sliced tomatoes.

3 Drizzle with ranch dressing.

4 Repeat the layers until you've used up all your cucumbers and tomatoes.

5 Top with mozzarella cheese.

Growing Up

Cucumbers grow on vines, so if you grow them on the ground, they can take up a lot of space. Don't let that stop you from trying them, though. Instead, grow them on a trellis. As the plants start to get going, use string or twist ties to tie the plants to the trellis. Every week or so, check your cucumber plants. Continue to tie them upward and the plants will continue to grow that way. Pretty soon, you should start seeing yellow blossoms on your plants and then tiny baby cumbers popping up from the flowers. It won't be long before you have regular-size cucumbers to eat. And best of all, by growing them this way, they don't get dirty or rot on the ground. Twist the cucumbers off gently when you're ready to pick them.

♻ RECYCLE IT:
Games in the Garden

Turn your garden into a game zone with these fun ideas. You don't need a lot of equipment. Just recycle a few items, and you'll have fun for hours.

Bubble Time

Difficulty: 🥄

Materials

- [ ] 2 cups of dishwashing liquid
- [ ] 6 cups of water
- [ ] ¾ cup of Karo syrup
- [ ] Kitchen utensils like jar rings, spoons with open slats, straws
- [ ] Shallow pan

1 Mix dishwashing liquid, water, and Karo syrup in a bottle. Shake the ingredients up and let settle for a few hours before using.

2 Meanwhile, search through your kitchen to see what might make a good bubble wand. The ring of a jar, a slotted spoon, and even a straw are all good options.

3 Dip your kitchen utensils into the bubble mixture in a shallow pan and then gently blow. It's fun to see what works best.

4 Store your bubble liquid in the refrigerator to extend its shelf life. It should last a week or more

Hula Hoop Toss

Difficulty:

1. Hula hoops are a fun garden toy. They don't take up a lot of space, and now you can turn them into a game, too. Buy hula hoops that are at least three different colors. If you already have some that are the same, just paint them.

2. You need three cloth squares for each player, so if you're going to have enough for two players, you'll need six squares. Make sure the squares for each player match, so the beanbags don't get confused. If you don't have matching fabric, sew patches or ribbons on the squares so it's easier to know which one belongs to each player.

3. Using a sewing machine or by hand, stitch up three sides of each cloth square.

4. Fill the squares with rice or beans, and then stitch up the final side. Don't overfill the bags. You don't need much filling to make the bags easy to toss, but try to make them as equal as possible. You don't want any one complaining that one set of bags is better than the other!

5. Write your home game rules on a piece of paper. Decide how many points tossing a beanbag into each hula hoop will be worth—some could be worth more than others! Decide how many different rounds you want to do.

6. Set the hula hoops out on the lawn, placing the hoop that is worth the most points farthest away.

7. Take turns tossing beanbags and keep track of the points. At the end of the game, tally up the score and see who's the winner.

Flowerpot Golf

Difficulty:

Materials
- [ ] Flowerpots
- [ ] Golf balls
- [ ] Golf clubs

1 Look for old containers or flowerpots in your gardening supplies. Another easy solution is to use the plastic pots that many of your plants might have come from the nursery in. They are just plastic and can definitely be used again.

2 Set out the pots across your yard, creating a little golf course. You can either sit them straight up so you have to chip in the balls, or you can lay them on their sides.

3 Borrow a few golf balls and golf clubs from your supplies. (If you don't already have these at your house, hit the local thrift store. You'll find a lot of extras for a few bucks.)

4 Get out a score card and take turns. See how quickly you can sink your ball into each pot. You get one point each time you hit the ball. As with regular golf, the low score wins in garden golf.

♻ RECYCLE IT:
Backyard Tunes

Wind chimes add life to your garden. The soft jingle blowing in the wind is perfect for a lazy day. Make these wind chimes by recycling common kitchen objects.

Other Wind Chime Ideas

- String up noodles
- Attach paper clips to one another
- Recycle tin cans
- Buttons
- Tools (wrenches)
- Shells
- Pinecones

Kitchen Wind Chimes

Difficulty:

1. Measure your strings so they are all about 24 inches long. You will vary the lengths later to add interest to your wind chimes.

2. Turn your colander upside down and thread the strings through the top, knotting the strings off so that there's about 6 inches on top and the rest on the bottom.

3. Gather up the strings through the top of the colander and make sure they are all the same length. (You will want to make sure these are even so it hangs level.)

4. Once you have all the strings evened out, tie them as a group to a shower curtain hoop. These hoops make great hangers.

5. Turn the colander over and thread beads onto the remaining strings. This is where you should vary your lengths to add visual interest to the chimes. The beads will add color to your wind chime, and they really glisten when the sun hits them just right.

6. Once you've beaded the strings, go ahead and tie off a knot, leaving a few inches of extra string below. This is what you'll use to tie the kitchen utensils.

7. When all of the strings are beaded, tie the kitchen utensils to the bottom of the strings. Use a variety of kitchen objects for visual interest, but stick with one kind of material for the best sound. If you have all wooden utensils, that will create one sound while all metal will create another. It's best to do tie the utensils on at the end because it'll make the colander a bit clunky to maneuver. Be sure to tie the strings tight.

8. Finally, it's time to hang your wind chimes. Find a good place in the yard where you can enjoy the chime's sound, then loop the shower curtain hoop on a shepherd's hook or branch.

MakE IT: Veggie Gardening Round II

Most people plant their veggie gardens in spring for a summer harvest, but that's not the only time to plant veggies. Keep your harvest going by planting another round of veggies in August. You can plant several "cool-season" crops. And don't forget pumpkins! The season isn't over yet! If you can time it right, you could have fresh veggies in your garden for six months or more!

Round II Veggies

Plant these Round II veggies as early as July or as late as September. Check the harvest date and your frost date to decide when is best.

- Cauliflower
- Broccoli
- Beets
- Carrots
- Rutabaga
- Onions
- Brussels sprouts

- Cabbage
- Lettuce
- Turnips
- Kohlrabi
- Spinach
- Swiss chard

Grow and Harvest

Difficulty: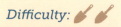

Materials

- ☐ Containers or garden space
- ☐ Soil
- ☐ Seeds

1 If you have some plants that have already produced for the season (lettuce, carrots, etc.), then it's probably time to clean out that garden bed or container.

2 After you've cleaned out the space, do a check on what needs to be added. Are you short on soil? Does the bed need to be repaired? Make any necessary adjustments before planting your next crop.

3 Check the back of your seed packets on harvest time, and make a chart. For instance, most pumpkins take 90 days to mature. So if you plant pumpkins right away at the beginning of August, they could be ready for Halloween at the end of October!

4 Plant seeds like carrots, lettuce, and radishes directly into the soil. Your local garden center might also have a second round of veggie plants available as well (or some leftovers from spring).

5 Early on, your plants need plenty of water to get established. They should germinate fairly fast (because of the warm, late-summer temperatures). Once they emerge, thin out the sprouts so they aren't crowded out.

6 For plants that take up more space (pumpkins and squash) look for space in your current flower garden. As long as the plants can still get sun, this is a good way to grow a second crop without having to till a new bed.

7 Keep up on your harvest. Monitor your summer-harvest veggies and don't forget to water and tend ones you planted more recently.

SEPTEMBER

115

GROW IT: Plants

Don't settle for plants that only bloom for a few days before they are done. Here are some more great perennials that will keep your summer garden beautiful for weeks.

Liatris

Difficulty: 🗲🗲

The Basics: Perennial, Zones 4 to 9, up to 3 feet tall

Grow It: These are fun plants to grow because the blooms are so fuzzy, and they stick straight up like a torch! Bumble bees and butterflies like fuzzy blooms, too. Add plants into your garden in spring. They do best in full sun to partial shade.

Top Secret Tip: If you plant liatris seeds, remember that they need a cold season before they'll bloom. These seeds will develop into rhizomes, which will need to be divided every few years.

Fun Fact: The top of these blooms often fade and look dead on the top. When this happens, just snip them off. They'll keep growing and will look great through fall.

Coreopsis

Difficulty: 🗲

The Basics: Perennial, Zones 3 to 8, up to 3 feet tall

Grow It: Coreopsis (also called tickseed) is a popular wildflower that has made its way into gardens all over the country. It does best in full sun and can definitely hold its own in dry conditions. The traditional flower shade is yellow, but there are lots of other options, too. Some varieties of coreopsis are considered annuals.

Top Secret Tip: Don't clean these plants out in fall. The foliage on the plants still looks beautiful in winter, and birds might even pick out a few leftover seeds to eat, too.

Fun Fact: It's the state wildflower of both Mississippi and Florida. Look for it growing wild in these and other states.

Clematis

Difficulty:

The Basics: Perennial, Zones 4 to 9, up to 12 feet

Grow It: This vine will twist and turn up to 12 feet long. It has huge, gorgeous flowers that can get to 5 inches wide. Plant in full sun.

Top Secret Tip: Clematis definitely needs a support to grow on. It does best on a thin support rather than thick branches or a heavy trellis. Try growing it against a fence or lean up a small trellis against your house or a garden shed.

Fun Fact: It's poisonous to dogs and cats, so if you have pets, don't let them start munching on this pretty flower.

Honeysuckle

Difficulty:

The Basics: Perennial, Zones 3 to 9, 3 to 10 feet long

Grow It: Most people grow honeysuckle along a trellis or fence, but you can also grow it as a groundcover. Plant in spring in full sun. Hummingbirds and butterflies love it.

Top Secret Tip: Some honeysuckle plants are invasive! Be careful: the best thing to do is check with your local garden center to find one that won't be too aggressive.

Fun Fact: You can taste honeysuckle, too. Just pluck a bloom from the plant and snip off the end. Then suck on the end for the sweet, honey-like nectar.

Blanket Flower

Difficulty:

The Basics: Perennial, Zones 3 to 10, up to a foot tall

Grow It: Blanket flower is a wildflower that grows all over the country. You don't have to do a lot of work with this one. Just plant in full sun about a foot apart. The blooms will last for months!

Top Secret Tip: Go ahead and plant these in late summer or fall (think discounted plants from the garden center). They'll overwinter well and be ready to bloom in spring.

Fun Fact: Also called Indian flower, this plant got its name because you can often find "blankets" of flowers growing in the wild.

Touch and Feel

In honor of fuzzy liatris, here are some more plants that are soft to the touch.

- Lambs' ear
- Dusty miller
- Cotton plant
- Bunny tail grass
- Cockscomb

PLANT IT:
Night Garden Plan

Night gardens—or moon gardens—are usually full of white flowers that look beautiful under the light of the moon. Try adding a moon garden to your backyard or just sprinkle in a few of these plants throughout your space. They'll glow all summer long.

Difficulty:

Plants: Nicotiana, moonflower, cosmos

The Basics: White flowers often stand out in the garden, making them beautiful to see by day *or* night. Think about this when you place your plants, so your night garden flowers have the best chance to grow and shine. Plant these varieties in full sun or partial shade. Moonflower grows as a vine, nicotiana grows just a foot or two, and cosmos grow several feet. Plant several of each variety within your flower bed.

Nicotiana: Also called flowering tobacco, the plants have lots of flowers. Make sure you get the white variety (they are also popular in red). They grow best in full sun to partial shade.

Moonflower: The blooms open in the evening and their bright flowers really stand out against the dark. These grow as vines (up to 15 feet), so you might want to add a trellis for them to grow up.

Cosmos: Make sure you find a white variety of cosmos. They are bright white and look good day or night. They grow tall in full sun. Mix them in with some pink cosmos, and then you can really see how they stand out at night.

Flowers That Bloom at Night

- Angel's trumpet
- Night phlox
- Yucca
- Evening stock
- Daylilies (like Midnight Splendor)

Nicotiana

Moonflower

Cosmo

You only need one or two squash plants to get a huge yield. And a little goes a long way in the kitchen too! Grab just two or three fresh squash for these recipes. You can use a traditional yellow (summer) squash or a butternut, too. Use whatever you have in your garden or the freshest variety from the local farmers' market.

Squash Kabobs

Difficulty: 🍴

Yield: 8 servings

2 cups squash in small, 2-inch squares

Kabob spears

Other garden fresh veggies

1 Soak wooden kabob sticks in water for several hours or overnight.

2 Preheat grill to a medium-low heat.

3 String fresh squash onto the sticks, and if you have different kinds of squash, alternate colors (also add other veggies if you like).

4 After you've threaded your fresh veggies on, drizzle with your favorite seasoning.

5 Try drizzling with ranch dressing, olive oil, or even butter; let your imagination be your guide.

6 Sprinkle with fresh herbs to top it off and then grill 10–15 minutes, rotating every 5 minutes.

Roasted Corn and Squash

Difficulty:

Yield: 6 servings

6 ears of corn

3 cups squash, chopped

2 teaspoons minced garlic

1 tablespoon fresh parsley

Salt and pepper to taste

1 Preheat grill at low to medium.

2 Husk corn and then remove the kernels by gently running a knife downward.

3 Place corn, chopped squash, garlic, parsley, salt, and pepper onto a large piece of foil.

4 Drizzle with olive oil and then wrap with another piece of foil.

5 Cook on the grill for 15–20 minutes, flipping halfway.

6 Remove from grill and let cool.

Barley and Squash Salad

Difficulty:

Yield: 6 servings

1 cup barley

2 cups water

2 tablespoons olive oil + 1 tablespoon olive oil

1 leek, sliced and using mostly the white part

2 cups butternut squash

¼ cup water

3 tablespoons minced parsley

1½ cups cooked black beans

½ teaspoon salt

¼ teaspoon ground pepper

2 tablespoons lemon juice

1 Cook barley in a small pot in 2 cups water until the water is absorbed.

2 Heat 2 tablespoons of oil in skillet over medium heat, and add leeks and squash.

3 Stir until lightly soft (about 10 minutes).

4 Add water and half of parsley and cook for another 2 to 3 minutes.

5 Transfer to a bowl.

6 Add barley, beans, salt, pepper, lemon juice, remaining tablespoon of olive oil, and remaining parsley.

7 Stir to combine.

Zucchini Bread

Difficulty:

Yield: 12 servings

3 eggs

1 cup oil

2¼ cups sugar

2 cups grated zucchini

3 teaspoons vanilla

3 cups flour

1 teaspoon salt

½ teaspoon baking powder

1 teaspoon baking soda

3 teaspoons cinnamon

½ cup chopped nuts

butter, shortening, or oil to grease pans

flour to flour pans

1 Preheat oven to 350°F.

2 Beat eggs.

3 Add oil, sugar, zucchini, and vanilla.

4 Beat slightly by hand.

5 Add flour, salt, baking powder, baking soda, and cinnamon.

6 Mix well, using a mixer if needed, and add nuts.

7 Pour into two loaf pans that have been greased and floured.

8 Bake for an hour.

Squash Tips

- Summer squash varieties include zucchini and crookneck. Winter varieties (which you plant in late summer and harvest in fall) include butternut and acorn. You can mix and match squash in recipes, as long as you cut them in the same small squares. It's fun to experiment.
- Plants produce a huge amount, so you don't need that many in your garden.
- Squash also grow on a vine. Train them to grow up (like cucumbers) or give them lots of space to crawl where they need.
- Summer squash only takes 45 to 50 days to mature while winter squash takes 70 to 100 or more. Look on the back of your seed packet and mark your calendar so you remember when you should expect to harvest.
- Grow squash in full sun and water regularly.

♻ RECYCLE IT:
Preserving Food

When vegetable gardens are in peak season, they often produce far more food than you can use. September is the perfect month to preserve your food by canning, making jam, and freezing your bounty. Even if you don't have extra, consider buying in bulk at the local farmers' market so you enjoy garden-fresh food in winter!

Canning Dill Pickles

Difficulty:

Materials

- [ ] Cucumbers, garlic cloves, jalapeños, grape leaves, dill seed
- [ ] Quart canning jars with rings and flats
- [ ] Large pan
- [ ] 1 quart water
- [ ] 2 quarts vinegar
- [ ] 1 cup pickling salt

1 Collect baby cucumbers, garlic cloves, jalapeños, grape leaves, and dill seed.

2 In quart canning jars, pack baby cucumbers with 1 garlic clove, 1 jalapeño, 1 grape leaf and 1 tablespoon of dill seed. Do not pressure-cook jars (some canning does require pressure cooking).

3 Bring water, vinegar, and pickling salt to a boil.

4 Pour mixture into packed quart jars.

5 Screw rings and flats on securely. Wait two weeks before eating. This is when the pickling will happen. Store and enjoy up to two years.

Freezing Corn

Difficulty: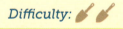

1 Fill up a large pot of water and drop in several ears of corn. Boil the corn for 10 to 12 minutes. Remove from water and drain.

2 Using a paring knife (be careful) cut the corn kernels off the ear.

3 Place the corn kernels in freezer bags. Fill the bag ¾ of the way full and squeeze out any leftover air.

4 Stack bags in the freezer flat. When ready to eat, defrost and heat over the stove. You can freeze other vegetables like beans and peas this way, too.

Oven-Drying Apples

Difficulty:

Materials

- Apples
- Oven

1 Preheat oven to 150°F to 200°F. Don't go too much higher than this or apples might get too crispy.

2 Wash, peel, and core the apples.

3 Cut apples into thin slices.

4 Place apples on cookie sheets and place them in the oven.

5 Drying the apples will take a total of 10 to 20 hours.

6 Periodically rotate the apples on different racks and turn, if necessary. When the apples are leathery, they're ready to be stored. They will keep for several weeks.

 # RECYCLE IT:
Harvesting Seeds

Now is the time to save seeds for planting next spring. If you can take time to learn how to do this, you'll save lots of money on next year's garden. You could even use seeds from your garden as gifts for family and friends!

It's in the Bag

Difficulty:

Materials
- Paper bag
- Seed heads
- Veggies
- Small bag to store collected seeds

1 As your garden reaches the end of its blossoming and harvesting season, it's time to collect seeds to plant for next year. To start, make a list of all the plants in your yard (or a friend's yard) that you want to collect the seeds from. This could include flower seeds like cosmos or veggie seeds like cucumbers and peppers. You can pretty much try to collect seeds from any plant you have in your backyard.

2 For veggies, pull the seeds out of the inside (cucumbers, tomatoes, and peppers are easy to find) and put the seeds out to dry on a paper towel. After a few days, put the seeds in a container and save for next spring.

3 Collect the flowers you want to harvest by cutting off the flowers, saving 10–12 inches of stem.

4 Wrap a paper bag around the flower head and tie it with a string. Hang the flower upside down in a dry location.

5 Flower seeds take a little longer to dry. Leave them upside down like this for a few months. Then in winter, just shake the bag, open it, and pour out your new seeds. Now you're ready to plant in spring.

Seed Art

Now is a good time to collect seeds for mosaics. Head outside and see what you can find in nature. Or harvest some extra seeds from your vegetables. For instance, pumpkin seeds are nice and big. They work really well for an art piece.

- To do a mosaic, first come up with a design. You can take something already created or draw your own. Remember that some of the best mosaics aren't actual pictures but just patterns. Draw your mosaic design on your paper. Then separate seeds based on what you want to use where.
- Use a regular craft glue to hold your seeds in place. And if you have gaps in between, just fill in with more, smaller seeds.
- Try the mosaic seed method on picture frames, poster board, or on a small end table. Use a mosaic grout to help hold and seal the seeds in place. It will make a unique, personalized gift.

Make It:
September Flowers

Most people design and build new flowerbeds in spring, but there are several good reasons to do it in fall instead— you save money on supplies and plants during end-of-season sales, and if you do the work now you'll have perennials emerging in your new bed come spring!

Save Time and Money

The advantage to starting a new flowerbed in late summer instead of spring is that you don't have to wait an extra year for plants like coneflowers and black-eyed Susans to bloom. They will have their cold period in winter and will be ready to go next year.

Raised Bed

Difficulty:

Materials

- [ ] Garden hose
- [ ] Shovel
- [ ] Pavers or decorative edging
- [ ] Cardboard
- [ ] Soil
- [ ] Plants, especially end-of-season perennials
- [ ] Mulch

1 Using a garden hose, outline the shape you want your new flowerbed to be.

2 Take a shovel and cut in around the flowerbed shape. Remove the hose when you're done.

3 Place the pavers or edging into the ground where you've cut it.

4 Place a couple of layers of cardboard on top of the grass of your new flowerbed. This will help kill the grass over winter.

5 Next, fill your new bed with soil.

6 Add the plants to your new flowerbed and water well.

7 Cover the new bed with mulch. This will really help protect your new plants as colder weather moves in.

8 If you have any tender perennials, you might want to cover them even more over the winter with some straw or potato sacks.

OCTObER

GROW IT: Plants

These plants will look great this spooktacular month! A couple look great all the way through October, but you can actually plant a couple of them this month, too! Either way, they'll keep you busy as cooler weather approaches.

Aster

Difficulty:

The Basics: Perennial, Zones 3 to 9, 4 to 6 feet tall

Grow It: It starts off small, but grows big fast. Plant in full sun during spring a few feet apart. You could get hundreds of little blooms on a single plant, and they add great color in fall.

Top Secret Tip: Asters come in a lot of different colors, even a pretty blue shade! Ask someone at your local garden store for a cool one to try.

Fun Fact: Asters were named after the Greek word for "star" because of their shape.

Ornamental Grass

Difficulty:

The Basics: Perennial, Zones 4 to 9, 12 inches to several feet tall

Grow It: There are tons of different kinds of ornamental grasses. Fountain grass, blue fescue, and feather reed are just three different types you can grow. Plant in spring, and then give it a couple of years to get established. They really shine in fall and early winter.

Top Secret Tip: Put together a grass patch in your garden, growing 4–5 different ornamental grasses. Read the labels, and place them from tallest to shortest.

Fun Fact: The ends of ornamental grasses make great toe ticklers!

Tulips

Difficulty:

The Basics: Perennial, Zones 4 to 11, 12 to 36 inches tall

Grow It: Before the ground freezes, plant your tulips 4 to 6 inches apart. They should be in a sunny location. Even try planting some directly into your lawn for a fun surprise.

Top Secret Tip: Make sure you dig a hole deep enough for tulips. They need protection over winter.

Fun Fact: It's the third most popular flower in the world and is more than 500 years old!

Mums

Difficulty:

The Basics: Annual, 10–12 inches tall

Grow It: These are everywhere in late summer and fall. They don't mind cold nights, so they are a great flower for containers.

Top Secret Tip: If you can buy these early enough, you can split them up and get lots of little plants out of one bigger one.

Fun Fact: Japan loves this flower! They celebrate it every year in September during the Festival of Happiness.

Sedum

Difficulty:

The Basics: Perennial, Zones 3 to 9, 24–36 inches tall

Grow It: Look for this perennial at the garden center and plant in a sunny spot. Butterflies love sedum, especially in fall when a lot of other blooms are done for the year.

Top Secret Tip: Don't lose patience with this plant. It's green in early spring, but it won't start blooming for four months or more when it gets cooler!

Fun Fact: If you cut off a stem of this plant, you can root it and grow more. Try doing this early in the season and keep adding more plants to your garden for free!

Keep Growing

Just because it's October doesn't mean your garden is done for the season. With decent weather, you can have beautiful flowers well into November. So keep those plants watered. Here are some of the ten longest-lasting blooms around.

- Geraniums
- Pansies
- Zinnias
- Petunias
- Phlox
- Black-eyed Susans
- Yarrow
- Salvia
- Indian Blanket
- Impatiens

PLANT IT: Create a Spooky Garden Plan

You can have a spooky-themed garden in your backyard by planting these plants. Best of all, they all look great throughout summer and in fall, perfect for Halloween.

Difficulty:

Plants: Witch hazel, Japanese blood grass, Casper pumpkins, Dragon's blood sedum

The Basics: This spooky combo does best in full sun to partial shade. Center everything around a single witch hazel. Plant three to four Japanese blood grass and Dragon's blood sedum. Then plant your Casper pumpkins near the middle because they'll grow outward. Remember it's best to plant these in early summer, and then they'll look great in early October.

Witch hazel. This shrub/small tree grows in most of North America. It has bright yellow blooms and leaves during fall.

Japanese blood grass. Grasses look great in the fall, and this one lives up to its name, turning a deep red color on the tips. It's a must for a spooky garden.

Casper pumpkin. This pumpkin get its name from that friendly ghost, Casper. They are nearly pure white and are fun to grow. Don't forget to start them in June or July so they'll be ready for decorating in October.

Dragon's blood sedum. Sedum is one of the best plants for fall. They love cool weather and the blooms really start to look great around September and October.

Creepy Plants

Find more creepy plants by doing a search online or checking out a good plant book from the library. For example, try searching for the word witch or Dracula. You might try finding black-themed plants, too!

Witch hazel

Japanese blood grass

Casper pumpkins

Dragon's blood sedum

EAT IT:
Yummy Pumpkin Goop

A little bit of pumpkin goes a long way. When you go to pick out your jack-o-lantern, grab an extra one to make pumpkin purée. Then try out a few of these yummy recipes!

Pumpkin Purée

Difficulty:

Yield: You can get about a pound of purée per pound of pumpkin.

1 pumpkin, smaller ones work better for purée

1 Preheat the oven to 350°F.

2 Cut the top off of the pumpkin. Clean out all the seeds and pumpkin guts.

3 Slice pumpkin into several pieces.

4 Place the pieces on a cookie sheet and bake for about 45 minutes or until it's soft when you poke it with a fork.

5 Take it out of the oven and remove the pumpkin skin (it should come off easily).

6 Use a food processor to blend the pumpkin a few pieces at a time until it is blended into a purée. Store in jars or plastic bags.

Pumpkin Pancakes

Difficulty:

Yield: 8 servings

2 cups all-purpose flour

2 tablespoons packed brown sugar

1 tablespoon baking powder

1¼ teaspoons pumpkin pie spice

1 teaspoon salt

1¾ cups milk

½ cup pumpkin purée

1 large egg

2 tablespoons vegetable oil

Chopped nuts (optional)

1 Combine flour, brown sugar, baking powder, pumpkin pie spice, and salt in large bowl.

2 Combine milk, pumpkin, egg, and vegetable oil in small bowl. Mix well, and add to flour mixture.

3 Stir just until moistened (batter may be a little lumpy).

4 Heat griddle or skillet over medium heat; brush lightly with vegetable oil.

5 Pour ¼ cup batter onto hot griddle; cook until bubbles begin to burst.

6 Turn and continue cooking 1 to 2 minutes.

7 Repeat with remaining batter.

8 Serve with maple syrup and nuts.

Spiced Pumpkin Seeds

Difficulty:

Yield: 4 servings

1½ cups sugar

¼ teaspoon salt

¼ to ½ teaspoon cinnamon

6 tablespoons milk

1½ cups dried pumpkin seeds

½ teaspoon vanilla

1 Mix first four ingredients and cook slowly in a medium pan, stirring occasionally, until sugar dissolves.

2 Remove from heat; add seeds and vanilla.

3 Beat until mixture thickens and hardens.

4 Turn onto wax paper and quickly separate seeds with a fork to let dry. Once cool, give them a taste. Store in a plastic container for up to a week.

Pumpkin Bread

Difficulty:

Yield: 12 servings

⅔ cup oil

3 eggs

2 cups puréed pumpkin

2 cups flour

3 cups sugar

1 teaspoon soda

1 teaspoon baking powder

1 teaspoon salt

2 teaspoons nutmeg

2 teaspoons cinnamon

2 teaspoons allspice

½ teaspoon cloves

Shortening to grease pans

Flour to flour pans

1 Preheat oven to 350°F.

2 Combine oil and eggs in bowl.

3 Mix in pumpkin.

4 In separate bowl, combine all dry ingredients. Gradually stir into wet mixture.

5 Prepare pans by rubbing sides with shortening and dusting with flour.

6 Separate mixture into two pans.

7 Bake at 350° for 1 hour.

Saving Pumpkin Seeds

Pumpkin seeds are one of the easiest seeds to save, either to plant next year or to use as art. They might be a little gooey when they first come out, but clean them up and be creative!

♻ RECYCLE IT: Creative Faces

Everyone *carves* pumpkins, but how about trying something new? Use fun things from your backyard to decorate your pumpkin this year.

Decorating a Pumpkin

Difficulty: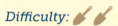

Materials
- [ ] Pumpkin
- [ ] Glue
- [ ] Leaves
- [ ] Twigs and other nature items

1 Go on a nature hunt in your backyard or around a local park. Gather items like fall leaves, acorns, twigs, flowers, pebbles, seeds and pinecones.

2 Look closer at the items you've gathered and think about how they could be transformed into your pumpkin's teeth, eyes, hair, etc. For example, small leaves might make great eye shapes and twigs might make great hair. Look at the list on this page for a few more ideas.

3 Sketch your design onto your pumpkin with a pencil.

4 Using strong glue or Glue Dots, start applying your objects from nature onto your pumpkin.

5 Once you have your pumpkin face complete, put it out for display. Keep in mind that it will be a little fragile, so you might want to keep it under an awning to give it more protection.

Household Pumpkins

Try recycling (or borrowing) some old kitchen and house-hold items to help decorate your pumpkin. Either glue on or use something like toothpicks to hold in place.

- Old forks. Bend for eyes or mouth
- Noodles. Glue on for teeth or hair
- Pan. Hat
- Milk jug. Cut into eye shapes
- Yarn. Hair
- Old socks. Cut up for hair or eyes
- Buttons. Eyes
- Milk caps. Eyes
- Foil. Cut and shape for a nose

Pumpkin Challenge

Here's a fun little activity to try at Halloween. Have a pumpkin fashion show! First of all, you need to set some rules. Can participants use anything or only recycled/nature objects? Once you have the rules set, give everyone a set amount of time to dress their pumpkin models. Once everyone is set, put some music on and let the fashion show begin. It's more fun if you have a prize. Once the show is over, let everyone vote for their favorite (but don't let them vote for themselves)!

A Touch of Nature

If you do still want to carve pumpkins, try a nature theme instead. A bird, flower, or butterfly are all great alternatives to ordinary pumpkin faces.

Make IT: Raise a Butterfly

Look for butterfly chrysalises and eggs this fall to raise your own butterfly just in time for migration! Most caterpillars and eggs will be on the underside of leaves. Make sure you're looking on the right host plants. For instance, monarch eggs and caterpillars are only found on milkweed. If you can't find any caterpillars, you can also purchase a butterfly kit.

The Circle of Life

Difficulty:

Materials
☐ Caterpillar
☐ Jar
☐ Milkweed

1 Puncture air holes in the top of the jar or container you'll use for your caterpillar's home. Don't make them too big or the caterpillar could crawl out!

2 Do a little research and find out what your caterpillar eats. For example, monarchs only eat milkweed, and black swallowtails need dill. (If you end up buying a butterfly kit and are raising a painted lady, food should be included. There will be instructions included, but you shouldn't need anything more than they give you.)

3 Once your caterpillar has turned into a chrysalis, it's time to watch and wait until it emerges as a butterfly. Then let it go so the cycle can continue!

Butterfly Life Cycle

1. First a butterfly lays its eggs in spring and summer and sometimes even in early fall. Remember some butterflies need specific plants (called host plants) on which to lay their eggs. If you want to plant a garden that supports butterflies from eggs to adulthood, find out what host plants are right for the butterflies you want in your yard.
2. Caterpillars hatch from the eggs a few days later. They start off very tiny. Then they molt (shed their skin) and grow bigger every day. They will molt several times before making a chrysalis.
3. After the caterpillar is finished growing, it makes a chrysalis. (It's not called a cocoon! That's for moths!)
4. Once the caterpillar is in its chrysalis, be careful not to shake it at all. Even though you can't see it, it's currently changing into a butterfly, so you don't want to disturb anything!
5. After 10 to 14 days, the butterfly should start to emerge. When it first comes out, the wings will be wet. It needs to dry for an hour or so. And then it's ready to fly, eat, and eventually lay more eggs!

Butterfly Plants

Want to attract butterflies? Butterflies will stop at any plants that are a good nectar source, but they need host plants to lay their eggs. Here are a few basic host plants to offer in your garden. For more suggestions, look for a butterfly book at your local library.

Butterfly	Host Plants
Black swallowtail	dill, parsley, fennel, carrots
Monarch	milkweed
Common hairstreak	hollyhock
Dogface butterfly	lead plant, false indigo
Cabbage white	broccoli, cabbage
Painted lady	hollyhock, sunflower
Buckeyes	snapdragons, toadflax, plantains

As monarch caterpillars grow, they shed their skin and then eat it!

Make It:
If They Only Had a Brain

It's the perfect time of year to build your own scarecrow. Just get some old jeans, a shirt, and something to stuff the body. Add a few accessories and voilà!

Do Scarecrows Work?

Farmers stuck scarecrows in their fields to scare the birds away. So did that really work? It did for some. Farmers set their scarecrows up on posts so they would blow in the wind, and the movement of the clothing—not the shape of the scarecrow—would scare hungry birds away.

Homemade Scarecrow

Difficulty:

Materials

- ☐ Old jeans or pants
- ☐ Rubber bands
- ☐ Leaves, hay or straw
- ☐ Old long-sleeve shirt
- ☐ Old pantyhose
- ☐ String
- ☐ Permanent marker
- ☐ Other accessories like a hat, gloves, boots, etc.

1. Using rubber bands, tie off the bottom of the jeans so when you stuff them, things don't fall out.

2. Take leaves, hay, or straw (whatever you have access to) and stuff the pants tightly. You don't want your scarecrow to get limp and fall over later.

3. Tie rubber bands on the end of the sleeves and stuff the arms. (Don't stuff the body of the shirt yet.)

4. Now for the hardest part. Take pantyhose and tie knots where the legs begin. Then stuff only the large part of the pantyhose (or the belly part) with leaves or straw. This is creating the head.

5. When the head is large enough, tie off the waistband of the pantyhose.

6. Before you stuff the body of the shirt, attach the shirt and jeans together by using string or even twist ties. You do this by making small holes around the bottom of your shirt and then threading the string through the hole and belt loops of the pants.

7. Take the legs of the pantyhose and run them down through the shirt, securing them to the belt loops as well. You'll have to decide where to tie them off based on where you want your head to sit on the shirt. Once the shirt and head is secure, finish stuffing the shirt (make sure all the buttons are secure).

8. Use a permanent marker to draw a face on your scarecrow. Or if you prefer, use a mask instead.

9. Finish the scarecrow by adding accessories like gloves, a hat, jewelry, etc.

10. Give your scarecrow a good post with a view of your garden. You could sit him on your front porch, up in a tree, or even just sitting out in the garden on a chair.

november

143

The growing season isn't over yet. A few flowers will still be in bloom, and it's a great time to add bulbs to your backyard beds. So roll up your sleeves and get ready to get your hands dirty before winter begins!

Daffodils

Difficulty:

The Basics: Perennial, Zones 3 to 9, 12 to 14 inches tall

Grow It: Plant daffodils in fall about three or four times deeper than the bulb itself, around 6 inches apart and in a sunny spot. Come spring, they'll pop up and be a bright spot in your garden.

Top Secret Tip: Make sure you don't plant these in shady spots. They'll never come up if they don't get at least 6 hours of sunlight.

Fun Fact: Are they stinky or sweet? Some people think daffodils smell like moldy bread, but others love the smell. You decide.

Knockout Roses

Difficulty:

The Basics: Perennial, Zones 4 to 9, 24 to 48 inches tall

Grow It: Roses have traditionally been difficult to grow, but the Knockout Rose makes it easier. Plant in a sunny spot where it has lots of room to grow. For rose bushes, be sure to follow the directions on the plant marker, digging a hold deep and wide enough.

Top Secret Tip: Find a plant for half price in fall, and then protect it over winter so it will have a good start in spring. You can cover it with a burlap bag or pick up a special rose cover from the garden center; they are pretty inexpensive.

Fun Fact: In fall, roses have little fruits called hips. You can pick them and even eat them. They look like little red berries.

Pansies

Difficulty:

The Basics: Annual, 6 inches tall

Grow It: Look for cold-tolerant pansies during fall. Sometimes called winter pansies, they can handle frost and work well in beds or containers.

Top Secret Tip: You can grow pansies from seed to save a lot of money. Use a germination mat to make it easier.

Fun Fact: Did you know you could eat pansies? You can. Just pick some petals and put them in your salad. Mmmmm.

Geraniums

Difficulty:

The Basics: Annual, 8–14 inches tall

Grow It: Geraniums are one of the cheapest plants to buy in spring. Plant them nearly any-where, even in partial shade. They will last all the way through fall.

Top Secret Tip: If you want to do a patriotic red, white, and blue container, get a blue pot and red and white geraniums. Then add a flag and you're done!

Fun Fact: Geraniums are sometimes used for deodorant. Keep the stink away!

Ornamental Cabbage

Difficulty:

The Basics: Annual, up to 1 foot tall

Grow It: Look for a pack of seeds at your garden center. Sprinkle them into the ground in summer in order to get fall and winter plants. They do best in full sun. You'll also find lots of these plants available for purchase in fall. Plant directly in the ground or in a container.

Top Secret Tip: Check the label at your local garden center, looking for an ornamental cabbage or kale that has the best cold weather resilience for your area.

Fun Fact: It might have the word cabbage in it, but you don't want to eat this! The leaves are tough and were developed for looks, not taste.

PLANT IT:
Welcome Wagon Plan

Mums, also called chrysanthemums, really are some of the best, most popular, and readily available flowers around in the fall. Grab a few of this favorite plant and create a colorful display. This huge display of mums on wheels will definitely welcome fall.

Difficulty:

Plants: Chrysanthemums

The Basics: A wagon or other large container with soil. Plant several different-colored mums. If you want to make quick work of this project, you can just place potted mums directly in the wagon. Try to use as many different colors as you can so you get a rainbow look! For a little extra insulation, add a little mulch around the edges of the containers. And if it gets especially cold one night, bring them in and then set back out in the morning.

Chrysanthemums: You can do so much with chrysanthemums. While most people think of them as a fall flower, they do great in summer, too. You can grow your own mums starting in spring, and they'll last all the way through frost. They are great to have later in the year because they hold up well in chilly temperatures. Mums always do best when they are in groups. If you're able to start your own mums from seed in spring or early summer, this is the most cost-effective way. But if not, buy as many mums as you can. To save money, join up with a friend and buy in bulk.

Chrysanthemum

EAT IT:
Onions with Attitude

Think you know all there is to know about onions? Think again! Onions often get a bad rap, but they really are pretty good if you give them a chance. Even if you don't like onions raw (like on a sandwich), they are a must-have ingredient in lots of dishes.

Pepperoni Dip

Difficulty:

Yield: 10 servings

8 ounces cream cheese

1 teaspoon garlic

6 ounces chopped pepperoni plus enough sliced pepperoni to top the pan before baking

8 ounces sour cream

4 ounces chopped green chilies

¼ cup diced onions

French bread, sliced

1 Preheat oven to 350°F.

2 Mix all ingredients together except bread.

3 Place mixture in pan. Top with pepperonis.

4 Bake for 20–25 minutes.

5 Serve with pieces of bread.

Sausage Balls

Difficulty:

Yield: 10 servings

1 (8-ounce) roll of sausage

1 cup shredded Cheddar cheese

1 cup Bisquick or similar baking mix

½ cup milk

1 egg

¼ cup chopped onions

1 Preheat the oven to 375°F.

2 Mix all ingredients together and roll into balls.

3 If the mixture feels too dry and crumply, use more milk. If the mixture feels too wet and slimy, add a little more Bisquick. It should feel moist but not too wet.

4 Bake until golden (roughly 20–30 minutes).

Taco Nacho Dip

Difficulty:

Yield: 10 servings

1 pound ground beef or ground turkey (browned and crumbled)

1 package taco seasoning mix

1½ cups salsa

1 pound Velveta cheese, cubed

¼ cup diced onion

1 Combine all ingredients in a slow cooker.

2 Cover and heat on low for 2 to 3 hours.

3 Serve with tortilla chips.

Chicken Tortilla Soup

Difficulty:

Yield: 8 servings

1 pound cooked, shredded chicken

1 can diced tomatoes

1 can enchilada sauce

1 medium onion, chopped

1 can chopped green chilies

2 teaspoons minced garlic

1 cup water

1 can chicken broth

1 teaspoon cumin

1 teaspoon chili powder

1 teaspoon salt

1 bay leaf

1 can corn, drained

1 tablespoon chopped cilantro

Tortilla chips, sour cream, shredded cheese

1   Place chicken, tomatoes, enchilada sauce, onion, green chilies and garlic in slow cooker.

2   Pour in water and chicken broth.

3   Season with cumin, chili powder, salt, and bay leaf.

4   Stir in corn and cilantro.

5   Cover and cook on low setting for 6 to 8 hours or on high for 3 to 4 hours.

6   Top with tortilla chips, sour cream, and shredded cheese.

Storing Onions

- Keep them in a cool, dark location around 50°F. Make sure they are in a dry spot as well.
- Many people will store onions in old stockings. Tie a knot between each onion so they aren't touching. This will prolong their life.
- If your location is too warm, the onions might try to sprout. Keep an eye on the onions and adjust as needed.
- Onions store for months. If you time it right, you'll hardly ever have to buy onions from the store again.

Fun with Leaves

It's not hard to find leaves this time of year. Just step outside, and you'll find thousands. Have fun with leaves this fall with some creative leaf projects.

Thanksgiving Placemats

Difficulty: 🔨🔨

Materials
- ☐ Glue
- ☐ Leaves
- ☐ Construction paper
- ☐ Contact paper

1 Glue leaves to construction paper, making a leaf collage.

2 Cover placemat with contact paper. This will help set the leaves and protect them against your plate, cups, etc.

Fall Wreath

Difficulty:

Materials
- [ ] Basic craft wreath
- [ ] Leaves with long stems
- [ ] Glue (optional)

1 Weave stems of leaves into wreath. Secure with glue, if needed.

2 Hang wreath on your door! It may not last very long, but it will still be festive.

Rubbings

Difficulty:

Materials
- [ ] Leaves with distinct veins
- [ ] Paper
- [ ] Crayons

1 Place the leaves on a piece of paper, vein side up, and then place another piece of paper on top.

2 Take the wrapping off of a crayon and, holding it horizontally, gently run it across the leaves. You should see the shape and veins of the leaves showing through.

Row of Thanks

Difficulty:

Materials
- [ ] Leaves
- [ ] Markers
- [ ] Large tapestry needle
- [ ] String

1 When your family and friends are gathered to celebrate the holidays, have them write what they are thankful for directly on the leaves with markers.

2 Thread a large tapestry needle with string and slowly add the leaves onto the string by pushing the needle through the top of each leaf one at a time.

3 When all the leaves are on, hang up near your Thanksgiving table. It's a fun and colorful way to see what everyone is thankful for.

Turkey Art

Difficulty:

- [ ] Large piece of paper
- [ ] Leaves
- [ ] Double-sided adhesive circles
- [ ] Markers or crayons

1 On a large piece of paper, stack leaves together to create a feathered look, using double-sided adhesive circles from the craft store.

2 When you have a good turkey body, add legs and a face with markers or crayons.

Leaf Journal

Difficulty:

- [ ] Leaf book from the library or online leaf guide
- [ ] Leaves from your backyard
- [ ] Construction paper
- [ ] Hole punch
- [ ] String

1 Look up each leaf in your collection and see if you can identify what tree it came from.

2 Make labels with colorful construction paper for each type so you remember which one is which.

3 Hole punch the edge of each leaf and tie with string to secure them in a journal.

MakE IT : Gardening in Any Weather

A terrarium is a miniature indoor garden. Think of it almost like a little dollhouse. It's a fun way to grow inside during the winter months.

Building a Terrarium

Difficulty:

Materials

- Glass container like a fishbowl or old aquarium
- Small rocks
- Indoor potting soil
- Terrarium-friendly plants, like succulents
- Miniature decorations

1 Clean out the glass container.

2 Create a drainage layer in the bottom of your glass container using gravel or small rocks/stones. If you can't find the right kind of stones, head to your local fish store. They have decorative rocks you can buy to use. You'll need about an inch of rock in the bottom of your container.

3 Once you have the bottom rocks in place, add soil along the bottom. Be sure to use an indoor potting soil instead of soil from your own backyard.

4 Add the plants, leaving room between them to fill in a few accessories as well. Make sure you know what kind of care your plants require. If you go with succulents, you don't need to water them much. But if you choose more tropical varieties, they like more humid conditions. Try to choose plants that are similar in their requirements.

5 Once your plants are in place, now you can decorate. Add miniature gardening details or little furniture throughout. This space is what you make of it!

✂ MAKE IT:
Multiply Your Plants

Give some of your annuals new life indoors by taking a cutting and growing them over the winter.

Indoor Cutting Nursery

Difficulty:

Materials
- ☐ Cuttings
- ☐ Glass jar
- ☐ Water
- ☐ Soil
- ☐ Small container

1 Look around your garden or a friend's garden and see what plants you want to take cuttings from. Easy choices include coleus or impatiens, but you can really try anything.

2 Once you find a good, healthy plant, pinch off a stem

3 Place the cutting in a jar of water so that the cut end sits in the water while the rest stays above. A small-mouth jar works great for this because the leaves of your cutting should hold the rest of the plant up. A clear jar will also let you see how your cutting is doing above and below water.

4 Wait 3 to 7 days and you'll start to see your plant growing roots. After roots have developed, plant in soil. Keep it in a small container over the winter near a sunny window. Come spring, you can plant in your garden and keep it going!

DECEMBER

GROW IT: Plants

December may be the darkest month of the year, but don't give up on gardening just yet. Incorporate it into your holiday decorations and you'll have an earth-friendly, beautiful display.

Amaryllis

Difficulty:

The Basics: Perennial, Zones 9 to 10, up to 1 foot tall

Grow It: Most people grow amaryllis around Christmas by forcing the bulb indoors. You'll find all kinds of amaryllis kits this time of year, and it's an inexpensive way to add some nice color in your house for the holidays. Keep your bulb watered and in a warm, sunny spot indoors. If you live in a warm area, plant it directly in the garden and let it grow!

Top Secret Tip: Be patient and don't overwater. The time it takes for an amaryllis to bloom can vary, so don't give up on it after a few weeks.

Fun Fact: Amaryllis bulbs can produce flowers for decades, but it is difficult to get them to rebloom, so most gardeners just toss them. If you want it to rebloom, cut off its leaves after it blooms, take outside in spring, and then bring it inside in August. It will need a few months of dormancy (in a cool, dark location) before you bring it back out to try to bloom again in fall.

Christmas Cactus

Difficulty:

The Basics: Houseplant, sprawling plant up to 2 feet tall

Grow It: This cacti plant has flat leaves and red, pink, or white flowers when it blooms. Look for it in fall at your local garden center. It's a houseplant that offers interest year-round, especially when it blooms around the holidays. Place it in a semi-sunny spot (not direct sun).

Top Secret Tip: You can easily propagate Christmas cactus. Take cuttings of stems when it's not in bloom and root them in soil. If you do this in summer, you should have some good plants to give to friends later in the year.

Fun Fact: Christmas cactus is from Brazil. Warmer climates like this don't always have traditional Christmas trees like we know. Christmas cactus is one of the things they would use to decorate around the holidays instead.

Dwarf Alberta Spruce

Difficulty:

The Basics: Perennial, Zones 2 to 7, up to 6 feet tall

Grow It: Dwarf conifers are very popular these days. Basically they are evergreen trees that are smaller in size, so they are more suited to the backyard landscape. Plant dwarf Alberta spruce in a large pot. Keep it outside in summer and bring it inside for winter. It looks a lot like a miniature Christmas tree, so you can even decorate it, too.

Top Secret Tip: They like sun. Plant it in a container that has wheels or in something else that is easy to transfer indoors and out.

Fun Fact: This small tree will eventually get to be 6 feet or more, but it will take several years to grow that tall. So enjoy it while it's small!

African Violet

Difficulty: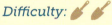

The Basics: Houseplant, 6 to 10 inches tall

Grow It: African violets are one of the few houseplants where you're almost guaranteed to get blooms. They like the same temperatures that most people do—not too hot and not too cold. They don't need direct sunlight, but they do need 8 to 10 hours of light a day.

Top Secret Tip: You can kill African violets fast by watering them too much. Don't use a watering schedule. Instead, feel the soil, and when it's dry to the touch, add a little water at a time.

Fun Fact: African Violets have a whole society! Check out the African Violet Society of America for tips on growing these pretty plants.

Poinsettias

Difficulty:

The Basics: Perennial, Zones 10 to 11, up to 2 feet tall

Grow It: Most poinsettias are only kept for a few weeks during the holidays. Go to your garden center for the best poinsettia selection—they will have more variety and healthier plants overall. You can choose lots of different shades including red, speckled, pink, white, and more. Remember that poinsettias can irritate your skin and make animals sick if they eat them. So keep them out of reach, if necessary.

Top Secret Tip: You don't have to toss this plant after Christmas. Keep it growing and then put it outside in summer. Some people can even get it to bloom again the following year.

Fun Fact: The color of poinsettias aren't actually flowers. They are called bracts (a lot like leaves). When the colors fade, the bracts go back to green.

PLANT IT: Red and Green Display Plan

Get in the spirit by adding a few red and green touches with your plants. You'll have a unique and festive display. Just get your plants at your local garden center this month, and you'll be ready to go!

Difficulty:

Plants: Miniature evergreen, redtwig dogwood branches, crabapple berries

The Basics: The best thing about this plan is that it's all things you can find at this time of year. Lots of garden centers sell miniature evergreens over winter, and then you can move them out to your garden in spring. Some stores also have branches of redtwig dogwood you can buy, too. And as for the berries? Get your scissors out and get outside to collect them!

Miniature evergreen: This is the centerpiece of your plan this month. Plant a miniature evergreen in a large container this winter. Consult your local garden center for recommendations on local varieties and care information.

Redtwig dogwood: The bright red branches of redtwig dogwood are readily available at your garden center. Use them to adorn your festive container. You can also bring them inside as decorations.

Crabapple berries: Borrow some red berries from your trees (like crabapple) or your shrubs and use them to brighten up your containers.

Miniature evergreen

Crabapple berries

Redtwig dogwood branches

eaT IT: Lovable Lettuce

Lettuce is one of those plants that you can actually grow indoors, as long as you have good light. Try growing lettuce in a container this winter and then harvesting your goods!

Corn Chip Salad

Difficulty:

Yield: 8 servings

1½ heads of lettuce, shredded

1 chopped tomato

1 chopped onion

1 6-ounce can olives, chopped

1 15-ounce can ranch-style beans

8 ounces Cheddar cheese

1 bag corn chips

1 16-ounce bottle Russian or Catalina dressing

1 Mix all ingredients except the corn chips and salad dressing.

2 When ready to serve, stir in corn chips and dressing.

3 The dressing should coat (but not saturate) the salad so use your judgment.

Tasty Taco Bake

Difficulty:

Yield: 6 servings

1 cup crushed nacho tortilla chips + ½ cup crushed nacho tortilla chips

1 15-ounce can chili with beans

1 small 4-ounce can chopped green chilies

1 6.5-ounce can sliced olives

½ cup sour cream

1 cup Cheddar cheese

2 cups shredded lettuce

1 Preheat oven to 350°F.

2 Spread 1 cup of crushed tortilla chips in an ungreased 8" square baking dish.

3 In a small bowl, combine the chili, green chilies and half of the olives; spoon over the chips.

4 Spread sour cream over the top.

5 Sprinkle with cheese and remaining chips and olives.

6 Bake uncovered for 10 to 15 minutes or until heated through and cheese is melted.

7 Top with lettuce.

Asian Lettuce Rolls

Difficulty:

Yield: 8 servings

6 ounces chicken-flavored ramen noodles

2 cups chopped chicken

½ cup green onions, chopped

2 tablespoons soy sauce

2 tablespoons vegetable oil

2 teaspoons Asian seasoning mix of your choice (check McCormick)

1 teaspoon garlic

½ piece of ginger, pressed

24 lettuce leaves

1 each red and yellow pepper, sliced

2 medium carrots, thinly sliced

Sweet and sour sauce to taste

1 Cook ramen noodles with seasoning according to back of package.

2 Drain and rinse under cold water.

3 Mix noodles, chicken, and onions in a medium bowl.

4 Combine with soy sauce, oil, seasoning mix, garlic, and ginger.

5 Toss to coat.

6 Place approximately ½ cup of mixture on a large lettuce leaf with 2 to 4 sliced peppers and 2 tablespoons carrots.

7 Roll lettuce around ingredients like a taco.

8 Drizzle with sweet and sour sauce.

Chicken Caesar Salad

Difficulty:

Yield: 8 servings

3 cups cooked shredded chicken breasts

1 head lettuce

1 cup red bell pepper strips

1 cup olive oil

3 tablespoons fresh lemon juice

2 teaspoons Worcestershire sauce

2 teaspoons Dijon mustard

A pinch of sugar, salt, and black pepper

1 teaspoon garlic

1 cup plain croutons

½ cup Parmesan cheese

1 Combine chicken, lettuce, and bell pepper in large bowl.

2 Combine rest of ingredients except croutons and Parmesan in a small bowl; stir well with a whisk.

3 Pour over salad; toss well.

4 Sprinkle with croutons and cheese, and toss gently to combine.

Tips to Grow Lettuce Indoors

- The most important thing is to make sure it receives plenty of light.
- Use a good potting soil mix, and make sure the container you're using has good drainage.
- Temperature is important, too. Make sure you don't put lettuce in an area that is too cold.
- Try microgreens. It's a good way to start growing lettuce inside, and you'll see results in only 7 to 10 days!
- Try different types. Some might work better in your area than others.
- Harvest lettuce when it's tender. You don't want it to get too big. You should be able to harvest your first leaves within a few weeks.

♻ RECYCLE IT: Gifts that Keep on Growing

Want an easy holiday gift that will hardly cost you anything? Give plants from your own backyard. Fall and early winter is a good time to divide plants before they settle in for cold temperatures.

Dividing Plants

Difficulty: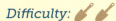

Materials

- [ ] Trowel or shovel
- [ ] Small rocks
- [ ] Potting soil
- [ ] Plants

1. How do you know if plants are ready to be divided? If they are overgrown or didn't produce quite as well as you expected this year, chances are it's time.

2. Use a trowel or shovel to divide at the root.

3. Put a layer of small rocks (like aquarium rocks) on the bottom of your container. This will help with drainage and is especially good for plants over winter.

4. When potting in a plant, always use new soil for the best chance of success.

5. Keep plants watered early on as they're trying to establish roots.

6. If keeping your plants inside over winter, most still need a dormant period. For perennials, this means putting them in a dark, cool location like a basement or garage. Then in spring, they'll be ready to go.

Giving Plants as Gifts

Difficulty:

1 Before you transfer the plants, go ahead and decorate the container. If you want to personalize it, use paint or markers. Or if you want to paint it, now is the time.

2 Follow instructions for Dividing Plants above. If you're just transferring them from your garden to a pot without dividing them, use the same instructions to prepare the drainage and soil.

3 Pot plants a few weeks before you're going to give them as a gift. You want to give them time to settle in before they go to their new home.

4 After the plants are in place, add some finishing touches. For instance, make a plant tag by printing off a picture of what the plant will look like during growing season and gluing it to a sturdy section of poster board. Just like the garden center, the picture of the plant should be on the front and the instructions for growing the plant should be on the back. Do a little research if you need to find out zone information, planting tips, etc.

5 To finish off the gift, add a pair of gardening gloves, a packet of seed, or a garden trowel. This will really make it complete, and the gardener in your life will love it!

✂ Make It:
Let's Get Personal

If you want a handprint keepsake, don't buy an expensive kit. Salt dough is simple to make and works like plaster. Best of all, you probably already have all the ingredients you need. These make a great holiday gift for a mom, teacher, or grandparent.

Handprint Plates

Difficulty:

Materials

- [ ] Flowerpot saucers large enough to fit your hand inside
- [ ] Salt dough
- [ ] Seashells and other personal materials
- [ ] Cookie sheet
- [ ] Plant stand or hanger

1 Mix up the salt dough according to the recipe here. When you have it to your desired consistency, press into your saucer and even it out.

2 When it's smooth on top, gently press your hand into the dough. Push down hard so you can make a good indention. The good thing about salt dough is it's hard to make a mistake. Even if you do, just mix it up and try again.

3 After you have a good handprint, press in other personal items if you wish. Things like seashells and craft letters will look nice around the handprint.

4 Salt dough will harden on its own, but it helps if you give it a little head start. Turn your oven on to 250°F and place your saucers on a cookie sheet. Bake for about an hour or until the dough hardens.

5 When the dough is hard, display the saucer on a plate stand or use plate-hanging hardware to show it off on a wall.

Salt Dough Recipe

Difficulty:

Materials (for 2 plates)

- 4 cups flour
- 1 cup salt
- 2 cups water
- Food coloring

1 Mix the flour and salt with the water and food coloring in a large bowl. A few drops of food coloring should do, but add more for a richer color.

2 Get your hands into the mix and really knead the dough well. You might have to add more water, as needed. When you get it to the right consistency, you're ready to mold.

3 When your dough is done, mold it however you like. Bake your creations at 250°F until they harden. Wash hands with soap, and the food coloring should come off.

Other Tools for Molding Salt Dough

- Paper clips
- Pencil
- Skewers
- Rolling pin

MaKe IT: Countdown-till-Spring Calendar

With an over-the-door shoe organizer and some creative garden items, you can create a nature-themed calendar that will keep you excited about your garden all winter long. It would even make a great gift. Give it to a gardener in your life, and he or she will have something to open every week until spring!

Ideas for Gardening Items

- Seed packets
- Coupons (help weeding, planting, etc.)
- Trowel
- Gardening shoes (split them up for different days)
- Plant markers
- Garden container
- Solar lights
- Plant food
- Seed catalog
- Flower calendar

If you're looking for a unique way to countdown to Christmas, this makes a great advent calendar, too.

A Gardener's Dream

Difficulty: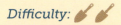

Materials

- [ ] Shoe organizer
- [ ] Gardening items
- [ ] Gardening quotes

1 First decide what your theme should be. Here, the theme is gardening, but you could also do another nature theme like birds (items for feeding and attracting them). For a gardening theme, make a list of all the items that could fit in the pockets. If items won't fit, you might consider just putting a coupon inside instead.

2 Most shoe organizers are inexpensive and have twenty-four slots, so you'll have room for two presents for every week of winter. Or look for an organizer that has more openings so you can make it last longer!

3 Look online or in a gardening quotation book for quotations for each spot in the organizer. Write them down and put a new one in each pocket for every day.

4 Add numbers on the outside of your shoe organizer. You can make your own or buy numbers at a craft store and attach them. Either way, this will be something you can use for years down the road. Every year, you could give it a different theme.

5 Once you have all the items ready, give your gift recipient the calendar along with a note that explains how it works.

You don't have to spend a lot of money on your presents. If you want to do all seed packets, you can either buy them in the off season or collect and give away your own seeds.

General Index

African violets, 156, 159
Alliums, 18
Amaryllis, 158
Animal garden, 46–47
Annuals. *See also* Perennials
  additional popular, 61
  basil, 3, 4, 5, 93
  begonias, 61, 156
  blue blooms, 90
  cilantro, 2, 77
  coleuses, 60–61, 75, 156
  coreopsis, 103, 116
  cosmos, 102, 103, 104, 105, 118, 119
  dusty miller, 90, 91, 117
  dwarf sunflowers, 48, 49
  fuchsia, 60
  geraniums, 131, 145, 156
  impatiens, 61, 131, 156
  marigolds, 61, 103
  moonflowers, 118, 119
  morning glories, 103
  pansies, 90, 91, 131, 145
  parsley, 2–3
  petunias, 60, 62–63
  reseeding themselves, 103
  salvia, 90, 91, 103, 131
  spider flowers (cleome), 102, 103
  sunflowers, 48, 49, 102–3
  zinnias, 48, 49, 103, 104, 105
April, 45–58
  Eat It recipes, 50–52
  Grow It: Plants, 46–47
  Make It, 57–58
  Plant It, 48–49
  Recycle It, 53–56
Asters, 130
August, 101–14
  Eat It recipes, 106–7
  Grow It: Plants, 102–3
  Make It, 113–14
  Plant It, 104–5
  Recycle It, 108–12
Azaleas, 35

Balloon flowers, 74
Basil, 3, 4, 5, 93
Basket of birdseed, 26
Bay leaves, 4
Bee balm, 89
Begonias, 61, 156
Berries, red, 160, 161
Birdbaths, 28–29
Birdhouses, 30–32
Birds
  basket of birdseed, 26
  food for, 26–27
  homes for, 30–32
  kitchen faucet birdbath, 29
  scarecrows and, 141–42
  wastebasket birdbath, 28
  water for, 28–29
Black-eyed Susans, 88, 131
Blanket flower, 117
Bleeding hearts, 20, 21, 75
Blue blooms, 90
Bookmarks, 9
Brushes and stamps, plant, 86
Bubble time, 108
Bug hunt, 81–82
Bulbs. *See* Perennials
Bulletin board, gardener's, 69
Butterflies
  life cycle, 140
  plants to attract, 140
  raising, 139–40
Butterfly weed, 46

Cabbage, ornamental, 145
Caladiums, 19, 20, 21, 75
Calendar, countdown-till-spring, 171–72
Candles
  do-it-yourself herb, 12–13
  gel for, 13
Canning dill pickles, 123
Cardboard birdhouses, 32
Cards
  garden, 99
  Valentine, 10
Carrots, 50–52
Casper pumpkin, 132
Catmint, 46
Chalkboard stepping stones, 57–58
Christmas cactus, 158
Chrysanthemums (mums), 131, 146, 147, 156
Cilantro, 2, 76, 77
Clematis, 117
Cleome. *See* Spider flowers (cleome)
Coleuses, 60–61, 75, 156
Columbines, 75
Compost bin, 83–84
Container gardens
  creative and DIY containers, 54–56
  general guidelines, 44
  patriotic display plan, 90–91
  personalizing containers, 71–72
  skirt for containers, 97
  thumbprint flowerpots, 72
  veggies in small spaces, 44
  welcome wagon plan, 146–47
Coral bells, 75

Coreopsis, 103, 116
Cosmos, 102, 103, 104, 105, 118, 119
Countdown-till-spring calendar, 171–72
Crabapple berries, 160, 161
Creepy plants, 132
Crocuses, 18–19, 36, 37
Cubbies, over-the-door, 69
Cucumbers, 48, 49, 106–7
Cuttings, multiplying plants, 156

Daffodils, 144
Daisies, 88
Daylilies, 74
December, 157–72
    Eat It recipes, 162–65
    Grow It: Plants, 158–59
    Make It, 171–72
    Plant It, 160–61
    Recycle It, 166–70
Decor, 98
    container skirt, 97
    garden tool greats, 98
    golf club flag, 95
    picture frame flower art, 95, 96
    pictures in the garden, 97
    scarecrows, 141–42
    tennis racket garden art, 66–67
Decorating/carving pumpkins, 137–38
Difficulty ratings explained, x
Dill pickles, canning, 123
Dividing plants, 166
Dragon's blood sedum, 132
Drying
    apples (oven drying), 124
    herbs, 3
Dusty miller, 90, 91, 117
Dwarf Alberta spruces, 159
Dwarf sunflowers, 48, 49

Eat It recipes by month. See also Index of Recipes
    about: topic description and icon, ix
    January, 6–8
    February, 22–25
    March, 38–40
    April, 50–52
    May, 64–65
    June, 78–80
    July, 92–94
    August, 106–7
    September, 120–22
    October, 134–36
    November, 148–50
    December, 162–65
Elephant ears, 47
Evergreens, dwarf/miniature, 159, 160, 161

Fall wreath, 152
February, 17–32
    Eat It recipes, 22–25
    Grow It: Plants, 18–19
    Make It, 30–32
    Plant It, 20–21
    Recycle It, 26–29
Flag, golf club, 95
Flowerbeds, building, 127–28
Flowerpot golf, 110
Flowerpot plant markers, 27
Flowerpots. See Container gardens
Flower projects
    bookmarks, 9
    frame, 11
Flowers. See also Annuals; Perennials; Trees and shrubs
    building beds for, 127–28
    in containers. See Container gardens
    pressed, 100
    veggies and, plan, 48–49
Forsythias, 34–35

Frames. See Pictures and frames
Freezing corn, 124
Fuchsia, 60

Games, 108–10
Garden phlox, 89
Garden plans. See Plant It
Garden tool decor, 98
Geraniums, 131, 145, 156
Gift ideas, 166–72
    countdown-till-spring calendar, 171–72
    handprint plates, 168–70
    plants as gifts, 166–67
Golf, flowerpot, 110
Golf ball bugs, 53
Golf club flag, 95
Grasses, ornamental, 89, 130, 132, 133
Green and red display plan, 160–61
Green beans, 64–65
Greenhouse, mini, 42
Grow It: Plants by month. See also Annuals; Perennials; Trees and shrubs; specific plants
    about: topic description and icon, ix
    January, 2–3
    February, 18–19
    March, 34–35
    April, 46–47
    May, 60–61
    June, 74–75
    July, 88–89
    August, 102–3
    September, 116–17
    October, 130–31
    November, 144–45
    December, 158–59

Handprint plates, 168–70
Harvesting seeds, 125
Heart garden plan, 20–21
Hens and chicks, 47
Herbs
    about: drying, 3
    basil, 3
    bay leaves, 4
    cilantro, 2
    do-it-yourself herb candles,
      12–13
    garden plan, 4–5
    nicotiana, 118, 119
    oregano, 3, 4, 5
    parsley, 2–3
    rosemary, 2, 4, 5
Honeysuckle, 117
Hostas, 20, 21, 74
Houseplants
    African violets, 156, 159
    amaryllis, 158
    Christmas cactus, 158
    dwarf/miniature
      evergreens, 159, 160,
      161
    poinsettias, 159
Hula hoop toss, 109
Hunting bugs, 81–82
Hyacinths, 19

Icon key, ix–x
Impatiens, 61, 131, 156
Indian blanket, 131
Indoors, growing plants. *See
    also* Herbs; Houseplants
    cutting nursery, 156
    dormant periods and, 166
    forcing blooms, 35, 158
    lemons, 8
    lettuce, 165
    starting green beans, 65
    terrarium for, 154–55
Irises, 19, 36, 37, 90

January, 1–16
    Eat It recipes, 6–8
    Grow It: Plants, 2–3
    Make It, 12–16
    Plant It, 4–5
    Recycle It, 9–11
Japanese blood grass, 132,
    133
Journal, leaf, 153
July, 87–100
    Eat It recipes, 92–94
    Grow It: Plants, 88–89
    Make It, 99–100
    Plant It, 90–91
    Recycle It, 95–98
June, 73–86
    Eat It recipes, 78–80
    Grow It: Plants, 74–75
    Make It, 85–86
    Plant It, 76–77
    Recycle It, 81–84

Key to icons, ix–x
Kitchen faucet birdbath, 29
Kitchen wind chimes, 112
Knockout Roses, 144

Lamb's ear, 47, 117
Leaf projects, 151–53
Lemons, growing, 8
Lettuce, 162–65
Lilacs, 34, 36, 37

Make It by month
    about: topic description
      and icon, x
    January, 12–16
    February, 30–32
    March, 43–44
    April, 57–58
    May, 71–72
    June, 85–86

July, 99–100
    August, 113–14
    September, 127–28
    October, 141–42
    November, 154–56
    December, 171–72
Make It projects
    birdhouses, 30–32
    chalkboard stepping
      stones, 57–58
    countdown-till-spring
      calendar, 171–72
    do-it-yourself herb candles,
      12–13
    flowerbeds, 127–28
    garden cards, 99
    handprint plates, 168–70
    multiplying plants, 156
    painting with natural
      paints, 85–86
    personalizing containers,
      71–72
    plant markers, 14–16
    plant stamps and brushes,
      86
    pressed flowers, 100
    raising butterfly, 139–40
    scarecrows, 141–42
    seed planting, 43
    terrarium, 154–55
    thumbprint flowerpots, 72
    veggies in containers, 44
March, 33–44
    Eat It recipes, 38–40
    Grow It: Plants, 34–35
    Make It, 43–44
    Plant It, 36–37
    Recycle It, 41–42
Marigolds, 61, 103
May, 59–72
    Eat It recipes, 64–65
    Grow It: Plants, 60–61
    Make It, 71–72
    Plant It, 62–63
    Recycle It, 66–70

Miniature flowerpot plant markers, 16
Monthly activities. *See specific months*
Moonflowers, 118, 119
Morning glories, 103
Multiplying plants, 156
Mums (chrysanthemums), 131, 146, 147, 156

Nicotiana, 118, 119
Night garden plan, 118–19
November, 143–56
    Eat It recipes, 148–50
    Grow It: Plants, 144–45
    Make It, 154–56
    Plant It, 146–47
    Recycle It, 151–53

October, 129–42
    Eat It recipes, 134–36
    Grow It: Plants, 130–31
    Make It, 141–42
    Plant It, 132–33
    Recycle It, 137–40
Onions, 76, 77, 148–50
Oregano, 3, 4, 5
Organization projects, 68–70
Ornamental cabbage, 145
Ornamental grasses, 89, 130, 132, 133
Oven-drying apples, 124
Over-the-door cubbies, 69
Over-the-door shoe organizer calendar, 171–72

Paint stick plant markers, 15
Pansies, 90, 91, 131, 145
Parsley, 2–3
Path, stepping stones for, 57–58

Patriotic container plan, 90–91
Peonies, 35
Peppers, 76, 77, 78–80
Perennials. *See also* Houseplants; Trees and shrubs
    alliums, 18
    amaryllis, 158
    for animal-themed garden, 46–47
    asters, 130
    balloon flowers, 74
    bee balm, 89
    black-eyed Susans, 88, 131
    blanket flower, 117
    bleeding hearts, 20, 21, 75
    blue blooms, 90
    butterfly weed, 46
    caladiums, 19, 20, 21, 75
    catmint, 46
    clematis, 117
    columbines, 75
    coral bells, 75
    coreopsis, 103, 116
    crocuses, 18–19, 36, 37
    daffodils, 144
    daylilies, 74
    dwarf Alberta spruces, 159
    easiest to plant, 88–89
    elephant ears, 47
    garden phlox, 89
    hens and chicks, 47
    honeysuckle, 117
    hostas, 20, 21, 74
    hyacinths, 19
    irises, 19, 36, 37, 90
    Knockout Roses, 144
    liatris, 116
    mums (chrysanthemums), 131, 146, 147, 156
    ornamental grasses, 89, 130, 132, 133
    poinsettias, 159
    purple coneflowers, 88–89

red star spikes, 62, 63
redtwig dogwoods, 160, 161
rosemary, 2, 4, 5
roses, 144
sedum, 131, 132, 133, 156
for shady areas, 74–75
Shasta daisies, 88
snowdrops, 18
soft to touch, 117
spring bulbs, 18–19
for summer blossoms, 19
sweet potato vines, 62, 63
tiger lilies, 46–47
tulips, 131
Petunias, 60, 62–63
Phlox, 89, 118, 131
Pictures and frames
    flower frame, 11
    picture frame flower art, 95, 96
    pictures in the garden, 97
Placemats, Thanksgiving, 151
Plant It
    custom plan, 10
    flowers and veggies plan, 48–49
    heart garden plan, 20–21
    herb garden plan, 4–5
    night garden plan, 118–19
    patriotic container plan, 90–91
    petunias plan, 62–63
    purple in springtime, 36–37
    red and green display plan, 160–61
    salsa garden plan, 76–77
    spooky garden plan, 132–33
    tall plants, 104–5
    welcome wagon plan, 146–47

Plant It by month
    about: topic description
        and icon, ix
    January, 4–5
    February, 20–21
    March, 36–37
    April, 48–49
    May, 62–63
    June, 76–77
    July, 90–91
    August, 104–5
    September, 118–19
    October, 132–33
    November, 146–47
    December, 160–61
Plant markers, 14–16
Plant stamps and brushes, 86
Plastic container birdhouses,
    32
Poinsettias, 159
Popsicle stick plant markers,
    14
Potatoes, 38–40
Preserving foods, 123–24
Pressed flowers, 100
Projects. See Make It
    projects; Recycle It projects;
    Grow It references; specific
    plant names
Pumpkin, 132, 133, 134–37
Purple coneflowers, 88–89
Purple in springtime, 36–37

Radishes, 22–25
Raised bed, 128
Recipes
    by main ingredient. See
        Index of Recipes
    by month. See Eat It
        recipes by month
Recycle It by month
    about: topic description
        and icon, x
    January, 9–11

February, 26–29
March, 41–42
April, 53–56
May, 66–70
June, 81–84
July, 95–98
August, 108–12
September, 123–26
October, 137–40
November, 151–53
December, 166–70
Recycle It projects
    bird food and water, 26–29
    bubble time, 108
    bug hunt, 81–82
    bulletin board, 69
    container skirt, 97
    creative and DIY
        containers, 54–56
    custom garden plan, 10
    decorating/carving
        pumpkins, 137–38
    decorations for garden,
        95–98
    dividing plants, 166
    fall wreath, 152
    flower bookmarks, 9
    flowerpot golf, 110
    fun with leaves, 151–53
    games, 108–10
    garden tool decor, 98
    gift ideas, 166–72
    golf ball bugs, 53
    golf club flag, 95
    harvesting seeds, 125
    hula hoop toss, 109
    kitchen faucet birdbath, 29
    mini greenhouse, 42
    organization projects,
        68–70
    over-the-door cubbies, 69
    picture frame flower art,
        95, 96
    pictures in the garden, 97
    plant markers, 16

plants as gifts, 166–67
preserving foods, 123–24
row of thanks, 152
rubbings of leaves, 152
seed art, 126
seed catalog art, 9–11
seed roll-ups, 41
seed starting, 41–42
shoebox storage solutions,
    70
spice jar seed storage, 70
tackle-the-garden box, 68
tennis racket garden art,
    66–67
Thanksgiving placemats,
    151
Valentine cards, 10
wastebasket birdbath, 28
wind chimes, 111–12
worm compost bin, 83–84
Red and green display plan,
    160–61
Redbuds, 34
Red star spikes, 62, 63
Redtwig dogwoods, 160, 161
Rock plant markers, 16
Rosemary, 2, 4, 5
Roses, 144
Rubbings of leaves, 152

Salsa garden plan, 76–77
Salt dough project and recipe,
    168–70
Salvia, 90, 91, 103, 131
Scarecrows, 141–42
Sedum, 131, 132, 133, 156
Seed catalog art, 9–11
Seeds
    arts and crafts with, 126
    harvesting, 125
    mini greenhouse for, 42
    planting made easy, 43
    roll-ups, 41
    spice jar storage, 70

Seeds—*continued*
   spider flower seed mat, 43
   starting, 41–42
September, 115–28
   Eat It recipes, 120–22
   Grow It: Plants, 116–17
   Make It, 127–28
   Plant It, 118–19
   Recycle It, 123–26
Shasta daisies, 88
Shoebox storage solutions, 70
Shrubs. *See* Trees and shrubs
Snowdrops, 18
Soccer ball birdhouses, 32
Spice jar seed storage, 70
Spider flowers (cleome), 102, 103
Spider flower seed mat, 43
Spooky garden plan, 132–33
Spruce, dwarf Alberta, 159
Squash, 120–22
Stamps and brushes, plant, 86
Stepping stones, 57–58
Storage and organization projects, 68–70
Sunflowers, 48, 49, 102–3, 104, 105
Sweet potato vines, 62, 63

Tackle-the-garden box, 68
Tall plants, 104–5
Tennis racket garden art, 66–67
Terrarium, 154–55
Thanksgiving projects, 151–53
Thumbprint flowerpots, 72
Tiger lilies, 46–47
Tomatoes, 76, 77, 92–94

Trees and shrubs
   about: planting, 35
   azaleas, 35
   dwarf Alberta spruces, 159
   forsythias, 34–35
   lilacs, 34, 36, 37
   peonies, 35
   redbuds, 34
   spring-blooming, 34–35
   witch hazel, 132, 133
Tulips, 131
Tupperware birdhouses, 32
Turkey art, 153

Valentine cards, 10
Vegetables. *See also Index of Recipes; specific vegetables*
   flowers and, plan, 48–49
   growing and harvesting, 114
   growing in containers, 44
   more sprawling plants, 48
   round II of, 113–14
   salsa garden plan, 76–77
Veggie can plant markers, 15

Wastebasket birdbath, 28
Welcome wagon plan, 146–47
Wind chimes, 111–12
Witch hazel, 132, 133
Wood plant markers. *See also* Popsicle stick plant markers
Wreath, for fall, 152

Zinnias, 48, 49, 103, 104, 105

Index of Recipes

Apples, oven-drying, 124
Asian Lettuce Rolls, 164
Avocados, in Holy Moly
  Guacamole, 92

Barley and Squash Salad, 121
Beans. *See also* Green beans
  Black Bean and Radish
    Soup, 23
  Corn Chip Salad, 162
  Tasty Taco Bake, 163
Beef
  Potato Casserole, 39
  Taco Nacho Dip, 149
  Tortilla Radish Rolls, 22
Breads
  Fresh Tomato and Basil
    Bruschetta, 93
  Oatmeal Carrot Muffins,
    52
  Pumpkin Bread, 136
Broccoli Radish Skillet, 23

Carrots, 50–52
  about: growing, 52
  Carrot Cake Icing, 51
  Carrot Pizza, 51
  Fresh Veggie Casserole, 65
  Glazed Carrots, 51
  Oatmeal Carrot Muffins,
    52
  Stacy's Secret Family
    Carrot Cake, 50
Chicken
  Asian Lettuce Rolls, 164
  Chicken Caesar Salad, 165
  Chicken Pepper Enchilada
    Dip, 78
  Chicken Tortilla Soup, 150
Cilantro, for salsa, 76, 77

Corn
  about: freezing, 124
  Corn Chip Salad, 162
  Roasted Corn and Squash,
    121
Cucumbers, 106–7
  about, 48; flower/veggie
    growing plan, 48, 49;
    growing, 107; harvesting
    seeds from, 125
  Canning Dill Pickles, 123
  Cucumber Bites, 106
  Cucumber Lasagna, 107
  Cucumber Salad, 107

Desserts
  Carrot Cake Icing, 51
  Lemon Snow Ice Cream, 8
  Lovely Lemons, 6
  Stacy's Secret Family
    Carrot Cake, 50
  Yummy Lemon Bars, 7

Green beans, 64–65
  about: growing, 65
  Fresh Veggie Casserole, 65
  Green Bean Grill Bites, 65
  Stir-Fry Green Beans, 65
Guacamole, 92

Lasagna, Cucumber, 107
Lemons, 6–8
  about, 6; growing, 8
  Lemon Snow Ice Cream, 8
  Lovely Lemons, 6
  Yummy Lemon Bars, 7
Lettuce. *See* Salads and
  lettuce

Onions, 148–50
  about: for salsa, 76, 77;
    storing, 150
  Chicken Tortilla Soup, 150
  Pepperoni Dip, 148
  Sausage Balls, 149
  Taco Nacho Dip, 149

Pancakes, 135
Pepperoni Dip, 148
Peppers, 78–80
  about: cutting into shapes,
    80; harvesting seeds
    from, 125; for salsa, 76,
    77
  Cheesy Pepper Pizza, 80
  Chicken Pepper Enchilada
    Dip, 78
  Fresh Tomato and Pepper
    Salsa, 79
  Taco Stuffed Peppers, and
Pizza
  Carrot Pizza, 51
  Cheesy Pepper Pizza, 80
Pork
  Sausage Balls, 149
  Slow Cooker Scalloped
    Potatoes, 39
  Tortilla Radish Rolls, 22
Potatoes, 38–40
  about: growing, 40
  Country Mashed Potatoes,
    38
  Fresh Veggie Casserole, 65
  Potato Casserole, 39
  Potato Salad, 40
  Slow Cooker Scalloped
    Potatoes, 39

Pumpkin, 134–37
    about: Casper, 132, 133;
        decorating/carving, 137–
        38; Halloween challenge,
        138; saving seeds from,
        136
    Pumpkin Bread, 136
    Pumpkin Pancakes, 135
    Pumpkin Purée, 134
    Spiced Pumpkin Seeds,
        135

Radishes, 22–25
    about, 22; tips for growing,
        25
    Black Bean and Radish
        Soup, 23
    Broccoli Radish Skillet, 23
    Radish Chips, 25
    Tortilla Radish Rolls, 22

Salads and lettuce, 162–65
    about: growing lettuce
        indoors, 165; lettuce and,
        162
    Asian Lettuce Rolls, 164
    Barley and Squash Salad,
        121
    Chicken Caesar Salad, 165
    Corn Chip Salad, 162
    Cucumber Salad, 107
    Potato Salad, 40
    Tasty Taco Bake, 163
Salsa, making, 76
Salt dough project and recipe,
    168–70
Sauces, salsas and dips
    about: making salsa, 76;
        salsa garden plan, 76–77
    Chicken Pepper Enchilada
        Dip, 78
    Fresh Tomato and Pepper
        Salsa, 79

Pepperoni Dip, 148
    Taco Dip, 94
    Taco Nacho Dip, 149
Sausage Balls, 149
Seeds, pumpkin. See
    Pumpkin
Soups and stews
    Black Bean and Radish
        Soup, 23
    Chicken Tortilla Soup, 150
Squash, 120–22
    about: growing, 122;
        summer, 122; varieties
        of, 120, 122; winter, 122
    Barley and Squash Salad,
        121
    Roasted Corn and Squash,
        121
    Squash Kabobs, 120
    Zucchini Bread, 122

Taco Dip, 94
Taco Nacho Dip, 149
Taco Stuffed Peppers, 79
Tasty Taco Bake, 163
Tomatoes, 92–94
    about: growing, 94;
        harvesting seeds from,
        125; for salsa, 76, 77
    Fresh Tomato and Basil
        Bruschetta, 93
    Fresh Tomato and Pepper
        Salsa, 79
    Holy Moly Guacamole, 92
    Taco Dip, 94
    Tomato Cups, 93
Tortilla Radish Rolls, 22
Turkey
    Taco Nacho Dip, 149
    Taco Stuffed Peppers, 79
    Tortilla Radish Rolls, 22

Vegetables. See also specific
    vegetables
    about: growing and
        harvesting, 114
    Fresh Veggie Casserole, 65

Zucchini Bread, 122

About the Author

Stacy Tornio is a Master Gardener living in Milwaukee, Wisconsin with her two kids and husband. She's been gardening with her mom ever since she could walk. As a kid, she even had her own produce stand with her brother at the local farmers' market. Stacy is the editor of *Birds & Blooms*, one of North America's largest gardening magazines. She also teaches kids' gardening classes to area youth. Stacy will try growing just about anything in her backyard—perennials, annuals, vines, veggies—but her personal favorite is growing cucumbers.

Photo and Art Credits

Watercolor illustrations by Joe Comeau.

Photos on pages 14, 27, 28, 31, 53, 58, 67, 68, 71, 85, 96, 98, 108, 111, and 169 by Tina Allen of lanaephotography.com and Scott Tornio.

fork © 123RF.com

1 © 123RF.com

v–viii © istockphoto.com/appleuzr

2 cilantro © bigstockphoto.com/DallasEventsInc

2 parsley © bigstockphoto.com/toriru

2 rosemary © bigstockphoto.com/JM Photography

3 oregano © bigstockphoto.com/Sylwia

3 basil © bigstockphoto.com/nsilcock

7 lemon bars © bigstockphoto.com/Andrea Skjold

9 iris © bigstockphoto.com/just4you

11 red flower © bigstockphoto.com/bluesee

12 herbs © bigstockphoto.com/BVDC

13 lavender © bigstockphoto.com/Irabel8

17 girl with birdhouse © istockphoto.com/nicolesy

18 allium © bigstockphoto.com/Sparkia

18 snowdrop © bigstockphoto.com/Wheatley

18 crocus © bigstockphoto.com/Ivonnewierink

19 hyacinth © bigstockphoto.com/AnnieAnnie

19 iris © bigstockphoto.com/buccaneership

22 sliced radish © bigstockphoto.com/iwka

24 radishes © bigstockphoto.com/KSLight

27 birdfeeder © istockphoto.com/AYImages

33 girl planting © bigstockphoto.com/Snark

33 forsythia © bigstockphoto.com/pmariann

33 lilac © bigstockphoto.com/AnnieAnnie

34 azalea © bigstockphoto.com/izanoza

34 peony © bigstockphoto.com/Shutter_bug

34 redbud © bigstockphoto.com/brendak715

38 potatoes © bigstockphoto.com/barney boogles

41 sprouts © bigstockphoto.com/Andy Dean Photography

44 planter © istockphoto.com/Funwithfood

45 family in garden © bigstockphoto.com/Anatols

46 catmint © bigstockphoto.com/Tainas

46 tiger lily © bigstockphoto.com/FaultySanity

46 butterflyweed © bigstockphoto.com/AardLumens

47 elephant ear © bigstockphoto.com/SCPhotog

47 hens and chicks © bigstockphoto.com/Carlo Taccari

50 carrots © bigstockphoto.com/sarsmis

54 bike © istockphoto.com/HeikeKampe

55 shoes © istockphoto.com/mtr

59 mother and daughter © bigstockphoto.com/brozova

60 coleus © bigstockphoto.com/Linkia

60 fuchsia © bigstockphoto.com/Jessamyn Smallenburg

60 petunias © bigstockphoto.com/kmf

61 impatiens © bigstockphoto.com/Sherri Armstrong

61 marigolds © bigstockphoto.com/ril

64 green beans © bigstockphoto.com/sarsmis

73 catching bugs © bigstockphoto.com/morganlstudios

74 balloon flower © bigstockphoto.com/L.Ann

74 day lily © bigstockphoto.com/Michael Shake

74 hosta © bigstockphoto.com/nkpics

75 coral bells © istockphoto.com/SkyF

75 columbine © bigstockphoto.com/rlinn3

78 peppers © bigstockphoto.com/Asento Photography

81 ladybugs © istockphoto.com/meadowmouse

82 worms © 123RF.com

83 compost © bigstockphoto.com/Mik122

87 girl eating watermelon © 123RF.com

88 coneflower © bigstockphoto.com/Michael Shake

88 shasta daisy © bigstockphoto.com/ponytail1414

88 blackeyed susan © bigstockphoto.com/NYPhotoboy

89 bee balm © bigstockphoto.com/pdb1

89 phlox © istockphoto.com/mountainberryphoto

92 tomatoes © bigstockphoto.com/Bedo

100 pressed flowers © bigstockphoto.com/marilyna

101 boy in sprinkler © 123RF.com

102 cosmos © bigstockphoto.com/lijuan

102 morning glory © bigstockphoto.com/pudding

102 spider flower © bigstockphoto.com/veronica1007

102 sunflower © bigstockphoto.com/mikdam

103 zinnia © bigstockphoto.com/gortan

106 cucumber © bigstockphoto.com/Digoarpi

113 helping in garden © bigstockphoto.com/PhotoEuphoria

115 dandelion © bigstockphoto.com/Gorilla

116 coreopsis © bigstockphoto.com/badboo

116 liatris © bigstockphoto.com/mlane

117 blanket flower © bigstockphoto.com/cpreiser

117 honeysuckle © bigstockphoto.com/D.H.Snover

117 clematis © bigstockphoto.com/Tootles

120 squash © bigstockphoto.com/bendicks

123 pickles © bigstockphoto.com/daci

126 seeds © bigstockphoto.com/MonaMakela

127 container garden © bigstockphoto.com/AnnieAnnie

129 boy with pumpkins © bigstockphoto.com/LisaTuray

130 aster © bigstockphoto.com/sergioazzini

130 ornamental grass © bigstockphoto.com/feierabend

131 chrysanthemum © bigstockphoto.com/matka_Wariatka

131 sedum © bigstockphoto.com/imblinky

131 tulips © bigstockphoto.com/Atlasmountain

134 pumpkin bread © bigstockphoto.com/Rojoimages

138 decorate a pumpkin © bigstockphoto.com/mbagdon

139 butterfly © bigstockphoto.com/CathyKeifer

141 scarecrow © bigstockphoto.com/nancykennedy

143 kids in leaves © bigstockphoto.com/sonyae

144 daffodils © bigstockphoto.com/vvvstep

144 geranium © bigstockphoto.com/songbird839

144 knockout roses © bigstockphoto.com/onepony

144 ornamental cabbage © bigstockphoto.com/tobkatrina

145 pansy © bigstockphoto.com/mypokcik

148 onions © bigstockphoto.com/joyfuldesigns

151 leaves © bigstockphoto.com/TRITOOTH

155 terrarium © istockphoto.com/MoniqueRodrigues

157 wreath © bigstockphoto.com/Sea Breeze

158 amaryllis © bigstockphoto.com/AnnieAnnie

158 christmas cactus © bigstockphoto.com/feierabend

159 spruce © istockphoto.com/Stella1964

159 african violet © bigstockphoto.com/AnnieAnnie

159 pointsettia © bigstockphoto.com/thepoeticimage

162 lettuce © bigstockphoto.com/Rainer Maria

167 plant as gift © bigstockphoto.com/

171 gardening tools © bigstockphoto.com/Iwona Grodzka

171 pink gardening tools © bigstockphoto.com/Chris_Elwell